The Penguin

HISTORICAL ATLAS of the MEDIEVAL WORLD

Andrew Jotischky & Caroline Hull

To the memory of Susan K. Hull

PENGUIN BOOKS

Published by the Penguin Group

Penguin Books Ltd, 80 Strand, London WC2R 0RL, England

Penguin Group (USA) Inc., 375 Hudson Street, New York, New York 10014, USA

Penguin Group (Canada), 90 Eglinton Avenue East, Suite 700, Toronto, Ontario, Canada M4P 2Y3

(a division of Pearson Penguin Canada Inc.)

Penguin Ireland, 25 St Stephen's Green, Dublin 2, Ireland

(a division of Penguin Books Ltd)

Penguin Group (Australia), 707 Collins Street, Melbourne, Victoria 3008, Australia

(a division of Pearson Australia Group Pty Ltd)

Penguin Books India Pvt Ltd, 11 Community Centre,

Panchsheel Park, New Delhi – 110 017, India

Penguin Group (NZ), 67 Apollo Drive, Rosedale, Auckland 0632, New Zealand

(a division of Pearson New Zealand Ltd)

Penguin Books (South Africa) (Pty) Ltd, Block D, Rosebank Office Park, 181 Jan Smuts Avenue,

Parktown North, Gauteng 2193, South Africa

Penguin Books Ltd, Registered Offices: 80 Strand, London WC2R 0RL, England

www.penguin.com

First published 2005
17

Copyright © Penguin Books, 2005
All rights reserved

Made and printed in Italy by Printer Trento Srl

ISBN 978-0-141-01449-4

Produced for Penguin Books by Haywood & Hall

Preface

The Middle Ages has an ambivalent place in contemporary culture. Unlike the well-defined periods to either side, it is often seen as a kind of waiting room between the much-admired Romans and the beginning of a recognizably modern society. It can seem alien, governed by religious certainties that we no longer take for granted, by warfare and cruelty, and by a comparatively low level of technology. But we can also find in the medieval world mystique and beauty, romance and adventure, and a pre-industrial simplicity now lost. Some of the our most enduring cultural icons, from Robin Hood and King Arthur to fairy tales, are medieval in origin. So too are many of the political, economic and cultural institutions of our society – from parliament and law-courts to universities. The intention of this book is to show that the medieval world was dynamic, innovative and creative; that the modern European world is dependent on forms of government and social organization shaped by medieval society, and that contemporary attitudes, beliefs and solutions to problems are not always so different from those of the Middle Ages. To understand Europe, we must understand the medieval world.

The format of an atlas imposes restrictions of space on the text that accompanies the maps and images. Inevitably, the choice of topics covered is selective. We have tried to provide a wide-ranging and representative introduction to the changing face of medieval Europe over a thousand-year period. If some regions are treated more fully than others, this reflects the prevailing state of knowledge and current trends in the historiography of medieval society. It is not possible to give a complete view of medieval Europe in equal detail, because there are still gaps in our knowledge of society in some centuries and some regions, particularly the north and east. We hope readers will forgive the omissions made to keep this book to a manageable length; we hope also that for those approaching the Middle Ages for the first time, this atlas will provide an accessible and lively guide. We would like to thank Simon Hall and John Haywood for their advice and oversight of the project, and Fiona Plowman for her careful and patient editing.

Andrew Jotischky & Caroline Hull
2005

Contents

Introduction

The historical atlas has never been more important as an educational tool. Many of us struggle to locate the changing geographical boundaries in today's world, let alone those of ancient civilizations or of the medieval world. Yet it is precisely these shifting borders and the collapse of one society before the might of another that have determined the confused shape of the modern world. Knowledge of the precise factors contributing to the early medieval division of the Balkan states between the Roman and Orthodox traditions of Christianity, for example, may not fully explain contemporary cultural and ethnic tensions, but without such knowledge a deeper understanding of more recent political and religious problems is impossible. Political and economic globalization, and technological advances in communications, have made a world with fewer geographical unknowns than ever before. To understand how this has come about, we need to fill in the gaps on our own individually-constructed maps of the past.

Age of Innovation

The period covered by this atlas saw a transition in Europe from ancient to modern society. The millennium beginning with the fall from power in 476 of Romulus Augustulus, the last ruler of the Western Roman empire, and concluding around 1500 with the first European exploration of the New World, was a period of dynamic innovation. The term 'medieval' suggests a cultural ebb between two great waves of change and development, yet this period saw the evolution of most of the major political, religious and social institutions that still dominate today's world. The concept of the nation state and the political philosophies behind it, systems of social organization, and the rights and expectations of the individual all achieved recognizable forms before the end of the Middle Ages. To this period the development of Roman and Orthodox Christianity and the rise of Islam can be traced. Alongside these burgeoning religious hierarchies, there evolved positive and, increasingly, suspicious attitudes towards people of other faiths. Regional allegiances, religious, cultural and ethnic, were codified across Europe, and, although many have disappeared, a great many more continue to exist. These are expressed through political affiliations, social attitudes and prejudices, in adages, proverbs and much-loved fairy tales. Not all of these medieval legacies should be looked upon favourably, but acknowledgement of all of these contributions must be granted.

A Persian illustrated manuscript showing Chingis Khan (c. 1162–1227) fighting the Tartars. Chingis Khan unified the Mongol tribes and created the largest land empire in human history, by conquering large parts of Asia.

Division of Maps

The maps in this atlas are divided into four sections, each with its own introduction. Three sections (Parts I, II and IV) are chronological, while Part III deals with the relationship between medieval Europe and neighbouring and peripheral peoples. Each map has been designed to stress an important aspect of the Middle Ages, be it a single event, such as the arrival of the Black Death in the middle of the 14th century, or a wider phenomenon that occurred gradually, such as the growth of international trade. Medieval Europe, perhaps inevitably, dominates here, while the various peoples of Western Asia and North Africa, because of their geographical proximity to Europe and their frequent direct influence on European culture, also feature prominently. East Asia, the Indian Sub-continent, sub-Saharan Africa and the Americas are mentioned only briefly, a fact made necessary by technical and design constraints and logical by (less defensible) historical precedents. Other parts of the world do not appear at all. Obviously medieval Europe did not develop in isolation, and future attempts to integrate cultural currents from elsewhere in the world will only lead to a greater understanding of European culture in the Middle Ages and the centuries since.

Reading Maps

The atlas as an educational tool has both benefits and limitations. Maps are like still frames from a movie; they freeze at a certain moment, allowing us to assess the state of things at a particular time and giving little away about what has previously occurred or what will follow. Like a timeline, a map lends itself to lateral connections (of the 'What else was going on at the same time?' type), while texts and lectures perform this task less effectively. The visual impact of arrows depicting, for example, the movement of peoples sweeping across Asia into Europe and the resulting tightly compressed Barbarian territories, almost hiding within the protective borders of the Roman empire, indicates concisely the situation in Europe as the Middle Ages dawned. Migration and the resulting political change, indeed, can hardly be understood without maps. Other phenomena, such as the spread of religions, the growth of urban culture and the development of universities, can be mapped at a remove; by noting the locations and dates of new foundations, one can build up a rough picture of social change.

Limitations of Cartography

Other topics, however, although still vitally important to our understanding of this period, lend themselves less well to study through cartography. Medieval attitudes towards the Jews, for instance, must be mapped carefully to avoid any implication that the increase in tension between Christians and Jews from the 11th century began as a European-wide movement, rather than as a series of localized reactions against disparate factors (including economic developments and overzealous preaching of the Crusades). Maps and atlases can never be perfect representations of historical reality, but they command an unparalleled capacity to cut across preconceived boundaries, whether political or historiographical. They remind students and experts alike that history is never tidy, and that because a certain region or culture has been neglected from one perspective, it should not follow that it did not play a part in broader cultural and societal developments.

Previous historical atlases of the Middle Ages have proved a valuable resource for this project. Although much of the information given here will be familiar to any student of the Middle Ages, we have tried to organize the material in order to emphasize connections. Each map and its text stand independently, but are best viewed as part of a whole rather than in isolation. The introduction to each section complements, rather than repeats, the information in the relevant map spreads, at the same time supplying the analysis that it was not possible to include in the individual maps and texts.

Finally, some caveats are necessary. Although each map is intended to stand alone, supplementary information has been provided to help readers get their bearings; for instance, political boundaries might appear on a map dealing with social development, or major cities on a map relating to the countryside. The same could be said of the accompanying pictures and quotes; they often provide a context for, rather than direct evidence of, the topic under discussion. The quotations, restricted to fewer than 50 words, have been freely translated to allow a meaningful point to be made. It is hoped that the dynastic tables and the timeline appended to the text will provide useful dates and overviews for those in search of the bigger picture.

This extract from Froissart's *Chronicles* depicts the battle of Sluys in 1340. Froissart composed his *Chronicles*, which are essential to an understanding of Europe in the 14th century, between 1370 and 1400 after he had travelled extensively throughout the continent. His lively text was accompanied by lavish illuminated illustrations.

Seventeenth-century engraving of Christopher Columbus (1451–1506) receiving gifts from the *cacique*, or Indian chief, in Hispaniola (Haiti) by Theodore de Bry. Curiously no portrait of the famed, but controversial, discoverer of America was made during his lifetime.

Timeline 440–770

WESTERN EUROPE	EASTERN EUROPE & BYZANTIUM	RELIGION & CULTURE	THE MUSLIM WORLD	WORLD EVENTS
c. 450 Angles and Saxons invade Britain. 455 Vandals from North Africa sack Rome. 476 The Western Roman empire falls; Odoacer becomes king of Italy. 481 Clovis I ascends the Frankish throne. 493 Ostrogothic rule of Italy begins.	441 The Huns agree a peace treaty with the Eastern Roman empire.			
	527 Justinian I becomes emperor of Byzantium. 535 The Gothic wars begin when Justinian sends Belisarius to drive the Goths from the West; Belisarius recaptures Rome (536). 542 Plague strikes Constantinople, killing over half of its population. 558 The Byzantine empire is invaded by the Avars.	*c.* 500 The Franks adopt Roman Christianity. 529 St. Benedict of Nursia founds a monastery at Montecassino.		
c. 568 Lombards begin their conquest of Italy.		589 The Visigoths abandon Arianism for Catholicism.	570 Muhammad, founder of Islam, is born in Mecca.	552 Buddhism is introduced in Japan from Korea. 581 Reign of the Sui dynasty begins in China. 600 Bantu influence grows throughout southern Africa; the Maya civilization at Teotihuacan is destroyed and Tikal becomes their new base. 618 China is unified under the Tang dynasty.
687 Venice becomes a Republic with a doge as its leader.	674–8 Arab forces besiege Constantinople.	*c.* 650 The Lombards convert to Roman Christianity. 664 The Synod of Whitby establishes Roman orthodoxy in England.	622 Muhammad flees to Medina; the Islamic calendar begins. 661 The Umayyad Caliphate begins, with Damascus as its political and cultural centre. 674 Arab armies reach the Indus river.	690 The Empress Wu, the only female emperor of China, assumes the throne. *c.* 700 Arab slave trade in Africa begins.
732 Arabs defeated by Franks under Charles Martel at battle of Poitiers.	700 The Volga Bulgars establish a monopoly on trade between Asia and the Russians until the arrival of the Mongols over five centuries later.		702 Islamic conquest of North Africa is complete. 714 The Umayyad Caliphate replaces the Visigothic kingdom in Spain. 750 The Umayyad dynasty ends; the Abbasid dynasty is established at Baghdad. 756 Abd al-Rahman founds a breakaway Umayyad Caliphate in Spain.	
c. 765 In England, the penny replaces the sceat as main coinage. 768 Pepin III dies and the Frankish kingdom is divided between his sons Carloman and Charles (Charlemagne).				

WESTERN EUROPE	EASTERN EUROPE & BYZANTIUM	RELIGION & CULTURE	THE MUSLIM WORLD	WORLD EVENTS
771 Charlemagne becomes sole leader of the Franks.				
784 King Offa of Mercia orders the construction of Offa's Dyke.				
795 The Vikings first raid mainland Ireland.				
800 Charlemagne is crowned emperor in Rome by Pope Leo III.			**800** Ifriqiya (Algeria) achievesindependence from the Abbasids.	**800** Islam has spread throughout North Africa; the Anasazi pueblo culture flourishes in North America.
810 Charlemagne dies in Aachen.	**813** The Bulgars besiege Constantinople, but are driven off.		**831** Muslim control of Sicily begins.	
840 Louis the Pious, son and heir of Charlemagne, dies near Ingelheim (in modern Germany).				
841 Dublin is founded by Viking raiders.				
843 Treaty of Verdun divides the Frankish Empire between the sons of Louis the Pious.				**c. 845** Buddhism is suppressed in China.
850 By this date the three field system of crop rotation has spread throughout Europe.				
860 Vikings discover Iceland. The Rus (Swedish Vikings) attack Constantinople.	**860** The first of three attempts by the Russians to capture Constantinple.			
886 The Danelaw is established in England.	**882** Kiev is established by the Varangians as a base for their trade route from the Baltic to the Black Sea.			
892 The Magyars settle the Danube basin.			**900** By this date, most of northern Spain has been reconquered by the Christian Asturians; the Islamic world is split between Sunnis and Shi'ites.	**900** The Classic Period of Maya civilization ends; isolated cities survive.
912 The Viking leader Rollo becomes the first duke of Normandy.		**910** William, duke of Aquitaine, founds the Benedictine monastery of Cluny.	**914** Egypt is seized from the Abbasids by the Shi'ite Fatimids.	**907** The Chinese T'ang dynasty ends; centralized government disappears until the the Song dynasty in 960.
919 Election of Henry I of Saxony to the German throne.			**945** Baghdad is captured by the Buwayhids, a Persian people.	
		966 The Poles adopt Roman Christianity.		
		975 The Hungarians adopt Roman Christianity.		
987 Hugh Capet becomes king of France; the Capetian dynasty reigns until 1328.		**988** Kievan Russia adopts Orthodox Christianity.		
c. 1000 By this date the castle has become common in Europe.	**1000** By this date the Russians have thrown off Varangian domination and established a state at Kiev.			**c. 1000** The Vikings reach Newfoundland; Ghana in West Africa reahes its height; Chimu culture emerges in Peru.
1024 Boleslaw I the Brave is crowned Poland's first king.	**1025** Death of Emperor-Basil II the Bulgar-slayer; his reign marked the high point of Byzantine power.		**1032** The Caliphate of Córdoba falls; numerous Islamic states (taifas) take its place.	**1025** By this date the Punjab in India is under Muslim control.
1042 Robert Guiscard establishes Norman rule in Naples, Salerno and Calabria.				
1054 The Reconquista begins in Spain.	**1054** Power in Russia shifts from Kiev to Novgorod and Vladimir-Suzdal.			**1050** The Chinese develop block printing.

1061–1290

WESTERN EUROPE	EASTERN EUROPE & BYZANTIUM	RELIGION & CULTURE	THE MUSLIM WORLD	WORLD EVENTS
1066 William of Normandy defeats Harold of England at Hastings. **1072** Norman forces take Sicily. **1086** William the Conqueror commissions the Domesday Book, a survey of land tenure and assets in England.		**1095** Pope Urban II preaches the First Crusade. **1098** Robert of Molesme founds the Cistercians.	**1097** Western crusaders defeat the Seljuk Turks at Dorylaeum; Antioch will fall in 1098. **1099** Jerusalem is captured by the crusaders.	*c.* **1100** Gunpowder is used in China; Hopi Indians in North America begin to use coal for cooking and heating.
	1099 Crusaders capture Jerusalem from the Muslims	**1113** The Hospitaller Order is recognized by Pope Paschal II. **1119** The Templar Order is founded.	**1119** The Turkmen leader Il-ghazi defeats the Normans of Antioch at the Field of Blood.	
1130 Southern Italy and Sicily are united under the Norman Roger II. **1135** Henry I of England dies; civil war ensues, with Stephen of Blois emerging as king.	**1142** Emperor Manuel Komnenos takes power; his dynasty partially restores the power and influence of Byzantium. **1147** The Baltic Crusade is launched.	*c.* **1140** Gothic architecture is pioneered at St. Denis; Catharism spreads in southern France. **1145** Pope Eugenius III calls for a Second Crusade.	**1145–8** The Second Crusade is led by Louis VII of France and the emperor Conrad III. **1171** Saladin becomes Sultan of Egypt.	**1151** The Toltec empire in Mexico comes to an end.
1147 Afonso I, the first king of Portugal, seizes Lisbon from the Muslims.		**1170** Thomas Becket, Archbishop of Canterbury, is murdered by knights of King Henry II. **1182** Philip II Augustus expels the Jews from French royal lands.		**1175** Muslim leader Muhammad of Ghur begins his attempt to conquer India.
1180 Fall from power of Henry I the Lion, duke of Saxony.			**1187** Jerusalem is recaptured from the Christians by forces under Saladin. **1189–92** The Third Crusade: Latin territory in the East is reduced to a handful of cities.	**1192** In Japan, the title of Shogun is awarded to Minamoto Yoritomo. **1195** Aztecs settle in the Valley of Mexico. **1200** From this date vernacular literature increases throughout India; the Incas leave the Andes and enter Peru.
1204 Philip Augustus seizes the Angevin territories in France. **1215** King John of England is forced to sign Magna Carta.	**1204** Constantinople is sacked by the Fourth Crusade; Baldwin I of Flanders elected Latin emperor. **1219** Estonia is conquered by King Valdemar II of Denmark. **1237–40** Mongol forces sack Moscow and Kiev. **1240** Swedish forces are defeated by Alexander Nevsky of Novgorod.	**1209** St. Francis of Assisi founds the Franciscan order. **1215** The Dominican order is founded by Dominic de Guzmán.		**1221** Mongol forces under Chingis Khan invade India. **1235** In West Africa, the Kangaba state begins to create the Mali empire.
1241 Mongol forces invade Hungary. **1252** The Florentines begin to mint their own gold coin, the florin. **1261** The Byzantines allow Genoese traders into the Black Sea. **1270** Louis IX of France crusades in Tunis.	**1241** Despite victories at Legnica (Poland) and Mohi (Hungary), the Mongols retreat from Europe. **1261** Emperor Michael VIII Palaeologus returns to Constantinople having reconquered his empire from the Latin crusaders.	**1265** Dante Alghieri born in Florence. **1274** St. Thomas Aquinas, theologian and founder of Scholasticism, dies. **1290** The Jews are expelled from England.	**1250** The Abbasid dynasty falls to the Mamluks.	*c.* **1250** Christian missionaries are active in China. **1267** Beijing becomes the Chinese capital under the new Mongolian Yuan dynasty. **1290** The Sultanate of Delhi is established in India.
1282 Llewelyn ap Gruffudd is killed at Irfon Bridge by English forces.				

1291–1500

WESTERN EUROPE	EASTERN EUROPE & BYZANTIUM	RELIGION & CULTURE	THE MUSLIM WORLD	WORLD EVENTS
			1291 The kingdom of Jerusalem, established by Christian crusaders in 1099, falls to Muslim forces.	**1298** Marco Polo, a Venetian merchant, writes a description of his journey to the Far East. *c.* **1300** The Temple Mound civilization flourishes in North America.
1301 Andrew III dies, ending Árpád rule in Hungary.		**1304** Petrarch born in Arrezzo in Tuscany. **1309** Pope Clement V leaves Rome; the Avignon Papacy begins. **1314** The Knights Templar are suppressed following charges of heresy.		
1314 Battle of Bannockburn: the Scots secure independence from England			**1324** Ottoman Turks capture Bursa; it will remain their centre of power until 1361.	**1324** Mali emperor Mansa Musa visits Mecca; Mali is recognized as a great power. **1325** Aztecs in Mexico establish their capital at Tenochtitlan.
1328 Death of Charles IV the Fair, the last Capetian king of France. **1340** An English fleet defeats the French at the battle of Sluys; the Hundred Years War begins. **1348–53** The Black Death enters Europe; the population fall by as much as one third.	**1371** Byzantine emperor John V is forced to become a vassal of the Ottoman ruler Murad I.	**1377** The Avignon papacy ends when the pope returns to Rome; an antipope is elected in Avignon and the Great Schism begins.	**1354** Ottoman forces advance into Europe.	**1368** The Ming dynasty begins in China. **1390** The Great Binding Law establishes the nations of the Iriquois Confederacy in North America.
1403 Charging interest on loans becomes legal in Florence.	**1396** European crusaders are decisively defeated by the Ottomans at the battle of Nicopolis.	**1397** The Medici Bank is established in Florence. **1400** Geoffrey Chaucer, English author, dies in London. **1417** The Great Schism ends at the Council of Constance.		**1400** By this date Swahili trading centres in East Africa are reaching new cultural and commercial heights.
1429 The French raise the English siege of Orléans. **1434** Medici control of Florence begins with the reign of Cosimo I the Elder. **1450** The Sforza family seizes control of Milan. **1453** French forces defeat the English at the battle of Castillon; the Hundred Years War ends. **1471** The Este ducal dynasty begins in Ferrara.	**1453** Constantinople falls to the Ottomans.	**1450** Around this date the use of movable type for mass printing is perfected by Johannes Gutenburg, in Mainz.	**1453** Constantinople falls to Ottoman Turkish forces.	**1438** The Incas of Peru begin their great territorial expansion. **1441** Portuguese merchants begin to export African slaves into Europe.
1487 In Augsburg in Germany, the Fuggers' Bank is founded. **1492** Granada, the last Muslim stronghold in Spain, falls to armies from Aragon-Castile. **1494** The French king Charles VIII invades Italy.	**1479** In the treaty of Constantinople, Venice agrees to pay the Ottomans to maintain trading rights in the Black Sea.	**1475** Michelangelo Buonarroti is born near Arezzo. **1494** First evidence of Jews living in England since their expulsion in 1290. **1500** By this date printing presses all over Europe are mass-producing texts.		**1487** The Aztecs invade Central America. **1492** Christopher Columbus crosses the Atlantic. **1499** By this date Portuguese explorers have charted the west coast of Africa, opening a sea route to India. **1500** European exploration of South America is under way.

Part 1: The Early Middle Ages

Medieval Europe emerged out of the transforming Roman empire in the 5th and 6th centuries. The traditional view of historians influenced by Edward Gibbon (1737–94) was that the western provinces of the empire were overrun by waves of Germanic peoples in the 5th century, and that the deposition of the last Roman emperor in the West, Romulus Augustulus, in 476, marked the formal end of the empire and the start of the Middle Ages. This view was criticized almost from Gibbon's own time. The picture is far more complex than simply one of military defeat and political revolution.

The 5th-century emperors in the West had been all but powerless for two generations before 476, and dislocation of the western provinces from central rule was an ongoing feature of the whole 5th century. Beyond the political sphere, many questions remain about the nature of the 'fall' of the empire. Did the underlying economic trends that sustained the empire collapse at the same time as the Germanic invasions, or did a recognizably Roman form of commercial life continue beyond the 5th century?

It is indisputable that Roman culture formed the backbone of early medieval society; clearly, then, not everything Roman disappeared with the political change of regime. Most importantly, there was no single military defeat as a result of which the Roman empire crashed into ruins. For much of the 5th century, Germanic peoples fought against Roman armies, but the Roman legions were, by this period, themselves largely made up of 'barbaric' peoples allied with the Romans. The change of regime in 476 was a stage in the transformation of the political life of Europe, but it did not mark a revolution in government or political life.

The Barbarians

Since the 3rd century, the western provinces of the empire had made use of Germanic recruits to the legions. By the 370s, larger groups of such pastoral peoples – whom the Romans called by the Greek word 'barbarians', to designate people utterly alien to them – requested rights of settlement within the Danube frontier of the empire. This may have been because they wanted greater security from the threat posed by other tribes, or because they saw benefits in settlement within the agrarian economy of the empire. The Visigoths were granted a 'foedus', or treaty, allowing them the right to settle and cultivate Roman land, but the terms of the treaty soon broke down and the Visigoths turned against their protectors.

By 376, when the emperor Valens was killed at the battle of Adrianople, the barbarians had established themselves as a powerful military presence in the empire. Their status, however, was still that of federates, or allies, of Rome. The Visigothic king Alaric led his people from the Balkans to Italy, where in 410 he sacked the city of Rome in a show of strength against the emperor Arcadius, who had failed to pay his army. The Visigoths subsequently established their federate kingdom in southern Gaul and eventually moved to Spain. During the 5th and 6th centuries this trend continued with the settlement of other peoples – the Burgundians, Sueves, Vandals, Ostrogoths and Franks – in the western provinces. Of these peoples, only the Vandals, who conquered North Africa, failed to acculturate themselves to Roman society or to assimilate with Roman government structures. In the 6th century they were wiped out by an invasion launched by the eastern emperor Justinian.

A gold and glass fibula of Frankish workmanship dating to the 6th century. Germanic peoples like the Franks adopted Roman customs such as wearing a Mediterranean cloak fastened by a clasp or fibula. The use of ornamental fibulae signified the owner's wealth and status.

Most Germanic peoples wanted to integrate with Roman society because they appreciated the wealth and stability that organized literate government could bring. As the Ostrogothic king of Italy Theoderic (493–526) expressed it, 'All rich Goths want to be like Romans; only poor Romans want to be like Goths'. Theoderic himself, who had been brought up as a long-term hostage of the imperial court at Constantinople, not only admired classical culture but appreciated that culture was itself the product of the leisure brought to a society by stable government. Ruling Italy on behalf of a small military aristocracy, he employed a Roman civil service to govern as far as possible according to Roman norms. In less remarkable ways, the same was true of the Visigoths, Burgundians and Franks. For long periods, Romans, particularly the upper classes, lived the same untroubled lives their ancestors had done. The slow pace of transformation is poignantly captured in the letters of the 5th-century Gallo-Roman aristocrat, Sidonius Apollinaris, who recounts a leisurely round of country-house visits interspersed with fears for an uncertain future as the Visigoths sought to extend their authority throughout southern Gaul.

A folio from Bede's *History of the English Church and People*. In five books Bede (672–735) wrote an ecclesiastical and political history of England spanning from the time of Julius Caesar to the date of its completion in 731. Bede was a monk, scholar and poet who wrote many books on subjects ranging from scripture to music. He is known as 'the father of English history'.

Historians are divided about the origins of the Germanic peoples. The traditional theory is that they were pushed westwards from the central Asian steppes or the Baltic regions by pressure on their pasture lands from other barbarian peoples. However, this view is no longer universally accepted. One alternative view is that the westward movement was an invention of later generations of literate barbarians seeking to articulate a coherent national origin.

Roman Perceptions

A further problem with the traditional view is that distinctions among the various tribes were themselves the product of encounters with the Roman empire: in other words, it was largely the Romans who categorized them into tribal units according to their perceptions of barbarian customs and speech. In any case, strict ethnic boundaries between 'barbarians' and 'Romans' had ceased to exist even before the first 'foedus' was granted. Most of the Roman army was based on the frontiers where the legionaries intermarried with local women. The most striking differences were not between Romans and barbarians but between provincial frontier society and urban society. To the urban bourgeoisie, soldiers represented barbarism.

The first period of new settlement, roughly from the 4th to the 7th centuries, saw the emergence of new Germanic kingdoms in Britain, Gaul, the German provinces, Italy and the Iberian peninsula. If the political transformation of the Roman world through barbarian settlement was one of the main features of this period, the other was the deepening of the rift between the western and eastern provinces. Reforms to the government and the army in the 4th century resulted in a strong, centralized imperial government based in Constantinople. To the East Romans, the losses of the western provinces were seen as temporary setbacks, and in the mid-6th century Emperor Justinian invested heavily in the reconquest of North Africa from the Vandals and Italy from the Ostrogoths. The price of victory in Italy was physical destruction and human depopulation on a huge scale. By c. 600, trade with the eastern Mediterranean had all but ceased. The large-scale villa economy had shrunk and towns were abandoned for hilltop fortresses. Parts of Italy, particularly the south and the Adriatic coast, remained under the domination of Constantinople until the 11th century, but the cultural orientation of the peninsula had changed forever.

Gaul and Britain

The 6th century was also critical to the process of transformation in the Roman provinces of Gaul and Britain. In Gaul, the Franks achieved dominance over the other Germanic peoples under their king Clovis (481–511) and his Merovingian successors. The Visigoths were pushed across the Pyrenees into Spain, where they established a sub-Roman kingdom that lasted until the Arab invasion of 711. After the Roman legions withdrew from Britain in the 5th century, a series of native Romano-British rulers, perhaps including the shadowy figure who was later to be revered as 'Arthur', kept the invading Angles and Saxons at bay until the first quarter of the 6th century. By 597, however, Christianity, which had become an index of Roman culture on the continent, had disappeared and had to be re-introduced by missionary initiative from Rome. The Roman contingent in the British population also died out as unprotected villas and towns were abandoned in favour of ancient hilltop defences.

The unique spiral minaret of the Great Mosque at Samarra in Iraq. The brick-built minaret with its outer staircase rises to a height of 52 metres (170 feet) and was possibly influenced by earlier Mesopotamian ziggurats. Samarra was the capital of the Islamic world for a brief period (56 years) after the Abbasid caliphate moved there from Baghdad in 836. The city's artistic and scientific achievements remain legendary in Arab history.

The Persian and Arab Empires

The more populous, urban and prosperous eastern half of the empire, roughly from the Adriatic to the Euphrates, was threatened not by the rise of new peoples on its frontiers but by the resurgence of an old foe, the Persian empire, and, in the 7th century, its successor, the Arab empire. The Persians overran Palestine and Syria in the early 7th century, but in doing so overstretched themselves, and were decisively defeated by Emperor Heraclius (610–641). However, the contest for the Near Eastern provinces of the empire was more than purely military. The provinces of Syria, Palestine and Egypt had become dislocated from the imperial centre in Constantinople during the 5th and 6th centuries due to resentment of high taxation, the squeezing of municipal autonomy and a policy of enforced conformity with the religious orthodoxy upheld by the emperors. Partly as a result of this, the Arab invasions easily prised the Asian and African provinces from the imperial grip. In the 8th century,

Constantinople itself was threatened by Arab conquest, and only in the 9th century did a vigorous imperial dynasty from Asia Minor reassert Byzantine military might in the Balkans and eastern Mediterranean.

The evolution of Europe in the period *c.* 400–1000 was characterized by cycles of new settlement and assimilation. The first such cycle, which lasted until roughly the 9th century, saw the emergence of strong states based on military aristocracies whose heartlands lay in southern England and the areas of France and Germany between the Seine and Rhine rivers. These rural provinces had been of marginal importance in the Roman world, but in a society in which local markets and subsistence farming took the place of international trade, the use of this productive agricultural land sustained military followings that in turn maintained the ruling dynasties.

Charlemagne

The Frankish monarchy under the Carolingian dynasty of the mid-8th to 10th centuries dominated western Europe. Far-flung conquests made possible by the effective use of heavy cavalry brought in portable wealth in the form of plunder and tribute. The overwhelming strength of the Franks, however, also created the conditions in which a more sophisticated government could surface. The assumption of the title of emperor by Charlemagne in 800, at the invitation of the papacy, presupposes in itself an awareness of the imperial ideal. Charlemagne's government and that of his successor, Louis the Pious, were informed by an ideology of imperial authority that derived from the model of Constantine and the Christian emperors of the 4th century.

Carolingian government was the most literate and sophisticated since the 5th century, and the Anglo-Saxon government of the 9th and 10th centuries, which made use of the vernacular in law and bureaucracy, was no less advanced. Both were based to varying degrees on cultural and religious ideals. Charlemagne collected scholars at his court from all over Europe, including Alcuin from York and John Scotus Eriugena from Ireland. A revival of classical learning was encouraged as a deliberate government policy. His aim was a moral and pedagogical regeneration of Christian society, to be achieved by military means – such as the enforced conversion of the pagan Saxons – and by the extension of monasticism throughout his empire. In the late-9th century King Alfred of Wessex saw his defence of southern England against the Danes as the protection of Christian society against the forces of evil. His 10th-century successors used monasteries as agents of royal policy to counteract the power of local magnates.

The Early Medieval Church

One of the characteristic features of early medieval society was the relationship between rulers and the Church. As the senatorial aristocracy lost political power to the barbarians, they began to dominate the Church, and most 5th- and 6th-century bishops came from this social class. Monasteries, introduced into Gaul from the eastern Mediterranean in the early 5th century, similarly became an outlet for the preservation of both Roman and Christian values and ideals. Early medieval rulers, however, needed the support of the Church not only in order to legitimize their authority, but, because literacy was largely the preserve of clerics and monks, for the more practical business of government. Monasteries in fact became important landowners in their own right as they accepted donations and bequests from the secular laity. As the foundation charter of Europe's greatest medieval monastery at Cluny (910) asserted, those who were unable to lead a life of monastic perfection themselves could nonetheless benefit from their wealth to support those who were.

As landowning corporations, monasteries became politically significant. Kings in 10th-century England and Germany used abbots and bishops in preference to secular landowners as agents of local government. As clerics, they could make use of a literate bureaucracy; because they were celibate, they could not found dynasties and pass on the land owned by their monasteries or sees. The use of the Church by governments, which by the end of the millennium was normal throughout western Europe, sometimes resulted in a blurring of the lines between secular and spiritual power. Thus abbacies and bishoprics might be given to relatives of kings or magnates, even when the recipients were not themselves clerics. The Church could do little about this state of affairs because between Gregory the Great (590–614) and Leo IX (1049–1054) there were few periods in which the papacy exercised any authority outside Italy. At times popes could not even count on the respect of the city of Rome: Charlemagne's intervention in Italy in 800 was a response to a plea from the Pope, who had been mutilated by the Roman mob.

Viking Settlement

Charlemagne's empire fractured under the pressure of another cycle of new settlement in western Europe. From about the mid-9th to the mid-10th centuries, threats to established governments by pagan peoples appeared to come from all directions: from the north in the form of the Vikings, from the south in the form of the Arabs and from the Magyars to the east. The Arabs raided the southern French and Italian coastlines, and in 846 even sacked Rome. The Magyars, a highly mobile pastoral people who reached as far east as Burgundy in the 10th century, developed a reputation for particular ruthlessness. Of all three peoples, it was the Vikings, especially the Danes and Norse, who were to have the most lasting influence on the shape of Europe. After an initial phase of raiding from the end of the 8th century, they began from the mid-9th century to establish settlements in eastern England and northern and western France. By c. 900, much of England and northern France was settled by Danes who had converted to Christianity and who proved too strong for the native rulers to dislodge. Meanwhile, Norwegian kingdoms were established in the Orkneys, Western Isles, Iceland and eastern Ireland.

The political accommodations reached with settlers were similar to those made by the Romans with the Germanic peoples in the 5th century. Early medieval society was 'multicultural' in the sense that although kingship was understood to be authority over peoples rather than over territory, it could encompass many different peoples each governed by their own laws and following different social traditions. This meant that the concept of an exclusive claim to occupy a given territory was unknown. Although, as Bede (672–735), in his *History of the English Church and People*, argued, certain people were granted authority by God over others, but this rarely resulted in the ethnic cleansing witnessed in the 20th century.

This ceremonial throwing axe was found in the tomb of a Viking nobleman in Mammen, Denmark. Made of iron and inlaid with silver, the axe is engraved in a typical Celtic style. The Vikings inherited the axe from the Franks and it became a popular Viking weapon. The Mammen axe illustrates the Vikings' talent for combining art and war.

The 10th century was largely a story of political collapse. The public authority of the Carolingians fell apart, to be replaced by strong regional dynasties. In part this process was hastened by the Carolingian tradition of dividing the inheritance, which resulted in rival successions among the grandsons of Charlemagne. The treaty of Verdun (843) has typically been seen by historians as the birth of two separate states, France and Germany, distinguished by different languages and political traditions. However, the dislocation of regions from the centre was also a feature of the growing military weakness of the crown, and the evident inability of kings to provide for the defence of regions against the threat of the new settlers. Charlemagne had appointed those he trusted to govern large regions in the name of the imperial crown. As Europe had no cash economy, such agents of the crown, the counts, were expected to finance their operations from grants of land within the regions entrusted to them. However, at the death of a count, the king had to choose between either attempting to secure the reversion of such lands to the crown so that a new count could be appointed, or simply allowing the dead count's heirs to succeed to the same office. The latter, which was the path of least resistance and also took advantage of the existing relationship between the heir and the region, led inexorably to the expectation of landed nobility to the right of hereditary succession. The consequence was the gradual dwindling of central control from the regions. In a time of external threat, it was those who could provide defences against the raiders, rather than the crown or its appointees, who could control the regions. And so over the 10th century, political power tended to fragment in the Frankish lands.

Strong Kingship

In England and Germany, in contrast, strong centralized kingship emerged from the ability of kings to mount effective military leadership. The successful defence of Wessex against the Danes by Alfred and his successors at the end of the 9th century led to the domination of England by the

The Shrine of Charlemagne in Aachen Cathedral, Germany. Emperor Charlemagne made Aachen the capital of the Holy Roman empire in 768. He secured four great relics from the Holy Land for the city's cathedral, including the cloak of the Blessed Virgin and the swaddling cloths of the infant Jesus. Such relics added enormously to the prestige of his rule.

house of Wessex in the 10th century. In Germany, Otto the Great's decisive victory over the Magyars at Lechfeld (955) allowed him to revive imperial pretensions. By the end of the millennium, the German monarchy was the only institution with the authority and wealth to attract the attention of the true successor state to Rome – the Byzantine empire.

There is evidence that the new millennium was greeted with premonitions of the end of the world. Chronicles report phenomena that they could not explain except by reference to Domesday: an outbreak of the skin disease known as St. Anthony's fire in the 990s; the appearance of a dragon in the sky over Burgundy and the Rhineland in 1002; and blood raining from the sky in 1009. As the Archbishop of Canterbury, Wulfstan, warned in 1014, 'This world is hastening towards its end; that is why things go from bad to worse, as the state of the world deteriorates before the coming of Antichrist, when it will be dreadful and terrible far and wide throughout the world'. Millenarianism must not be exaggerated. Portents and signs are a feature of medieval chronicles. Moreover, Europeans were far from agreed when the new millennium would dawn because dating systems differed widely. But, although they could scarcely have been aware of it, great changes were imminent in the century after the millennium. By *c.* 1000, improvements in agricultural technology were beginning to encourage a rise in population and the cultivation of new lands in Europe. An age of expansion was about to dawn.

The Barbarian Kingdoms

Historians conveniently date the fall of the Roman empire to 476 when the last emperor of the western empire, Romulus Augustulus, lost his throne to Odoacer, a barbarian general. In reality the empire had been undergoing a complex transformation from as early as the mid-3rd century which would result in the emergence of a Europe whose cultural demarcations remain recognizable today.

"Why ... ask me to compose a song ... to praise ... that gluttonous barbarian who spreads rancid butter on his face?"

Letter of Sidonius Apollinaris

In land area, the Roman empire had reached its peak in the 2nd century, and by 476 it no longer included Dacia, Mesopotamia and the Agri Decumates, a small area south of the Rhine. Other outlying areas, including Britain, were effectively no longer under imperial control. A succession of weak emperors, economic problems and manpower shortages had severely weakened the empire and threatened the ability of the Roman armies to guard against invasion. The large size of the empire must also have created problems in maintaining control over so many different peoples, each with its own customs, language and laws. Over time, the distinction between Roman and non-Roman became blurred. The various barbarian tribes,

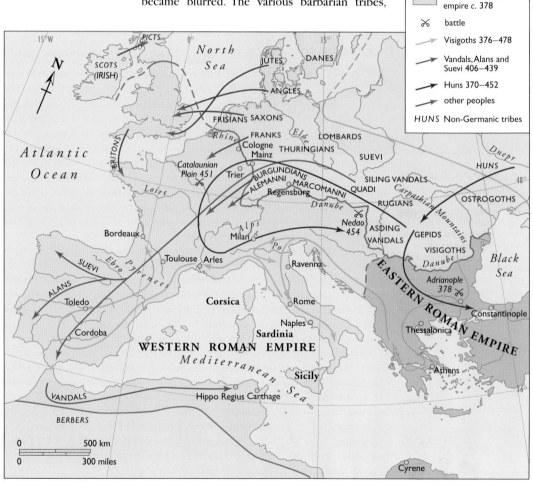

The Migration Period

- Germanic tribes
- Eastern Roman empire c. 378
- Western Roman empire c. 378
- ✂ battle
- → Visigoths 376–478
- → Vandals, Alans and Suevi 406–439
- → Huns 370–452
- → other peoples
- *HUNS* Non-Germanic tribes

sweeping into western Europe from the East in search of land on which to settle, certainly posed problems for the Roman administration and defence systems, but not an overall threat. There was, in short, no unified or organized 'nation of barbarians' as historians assumed for so many years.

The 5th century AD is the period of greatest tribal relocation in Europe. Among the barbarian tribes settling within the western half of the Roman empire, several stand out in terms of centralized control and large-scale settlement patterns. The Visigoths, settling parts of Gaul and the Iberian Peninsula, and the related Ostrogoths, ruling Italy and most of eastern Europe south of the Danube, are two of the most important. The Vandals, in northern Africa and southern Spain, caused some considerable problems to the Romans. The Franks, claimed as ancestors by both the modern French and Germans, would by 800 found an empire under Charlemagne, to rival the Western Roman empire.

The collapse of Roman administration in Europe in the late 5th century resulted in a redistribution of wealth and power among a group of ethnically distinct peoples who, in turn, intermarried and over the centuries formed a series of groupings with new sets of values, laws and traditions. Just as the barbarian tribes had never posed a unified threat to the Roman empire, neither would any of these original tribes emerge unadulterated to form a pan-European power base with imperial ambitions similar to those of the Romans before them.

A 3rd-century battle scene from the Ludovisi Sarcophagus, showing short-haired, youthful Romans in action against long-haired, bearded Germans. The Roman commander (centre) has been identified as Hostilian, son of the emperor Decius, who died in AD 252.

The Barbarian Kingdoms

- Germanic kingdoms and peoples c. 525
- Eastern Roman empire c. 525
- late Roman imperial capitals
- battle

Catholic Franks, under Clovis, defeat the Arian Visigoths

capital of Western Roman empire 402–76 and of barbarian kings of Italy 476–540

0 — 500 km
0 — 300 miles

The Conversion of Europe

By 600, with Roman political and cultural dominance gone and its territories overrun by a host of new peoples, Europe was in danger of losing the classical cultural identity which the Romans had bestowed upon it. For the next few centuries, and indeed throughout the Middle Ages, Christianity would provide the cultural, spiritual and, at times, political cohesion once offered by the Romans.

"While Clovis was still in the errors of his idolatry, he made war with the Alemanni.... He [Clovis] spoke thus: 'Most mighty God, whom my queen Clothilde worships and adores with heart and soul, I pledge you perpetual service, if only you give me now the victory over my enemies.'"

The Chronicle of Saint-Denis, I. 18–19

The Edict of Milan, issued by the emperor Constantine and allowing Christians freedom of worship, initiated the Christianization of the Roman empire. The conversion of parts of the Roman elite and the promulgation of Christianity by Roman administrators set Europe on the path towards conversion, but fairly quickly the Church gathered its own momentum. Charismatic individuals, some isolated holy men and women, others popular bishops and clergy, held great sway over local populations, while shrines devoted to holy relics and large monasteries whose inhabitants devoted their lives to spiritual salvation achieved renown across Europe. Impressive ecclesiastical complexes, such as cathedrals and monasteries, based on traditional Roman imperial structures, began to replace these on the nascent urban landscapes across the continent.

Paganism

Many barbarian tribes continued to follow their ancient pagan rites, and many citizens of the empire, that is the indigenous peoples of Rome's European territories, remained pagan for some time as well. Some barbarian groups had converted early on to Christianity, like the Visigoths, but their failure to embrace orthodox Christianity raised further obstacles to a simple conversion. Arianism, the brand of Christianity espoused by the Visigoths, was the heresy most commonly encountered in Europe during this period. Arian Christians believed that Jesus Christ, the son of God, could not have been divine as that state was reserved only for the Godhead. Once the movement towards Christianity had taken root, problems between groups subscribing to the variants began to surface. Aside from many heretical sects, the congregations led by the patriarchs of Rome and Constantinople respectively were increasingly diverging in their practices, and would espouse distinct forms of Christianity by the 9th century. By 700 Roman traditions and rituals were favoured by the vast majority of western European Christians; conversion there would now be solely to the church of Rome.

To those strongholds of paganism, Christian missionaries were sent. Early Christian missionaries from Italy, North Africa and Asia Minor had travelled north to indoctrinate the Germanic and Celtic peoples. With help from the newly-converted Irish and Saxons, Roman missionaries continued the job of converting the pagans remaining in western Europe.

The Kildalton Cross on the island of Islay in the Hebrides. It dates to the 9th or 10th century and is regarded as the finest Celtic cross in Scotland. Ancient stone crosses are the earliest symbols of the development of Christianity in Scotland.

The Slavic tribes in the east were under pressure from both the Roman and Greek churches. The conversion of the Serbians, Bulgarians and Russians to Greek (Orthodox) Christianity in the 9th and 10th centuries was a major setback for the Roman church and consequently for the social and political cohesion of Europe as a whole. By 1000, Christianity was being practised everywhere in Europe, although it would not be until the Later Middle Ages that the final, formal conversions took place.

The conversion of Europe ostensibly to a single set of religious beliefs, important as perhaps this was for general social cohesion, was not the most important result of the broad uptake of Christianity in the Late Antique and Early Medieval periods. What mass conversion did, at least for western and central Europe, was provide a stable, legitimate socio-religious hierarchy which could replace the crumbling power structures of the Western Roman empire. Although real political power would not be wielded in any organized way by the papacy and the ecclesiastical structure of the Roman Church much before the 11th century, the Church can be seen as directly replacing the Roman empire as the main vehicle for the development of the classical traditions which form such a large part of the modern European heritage.

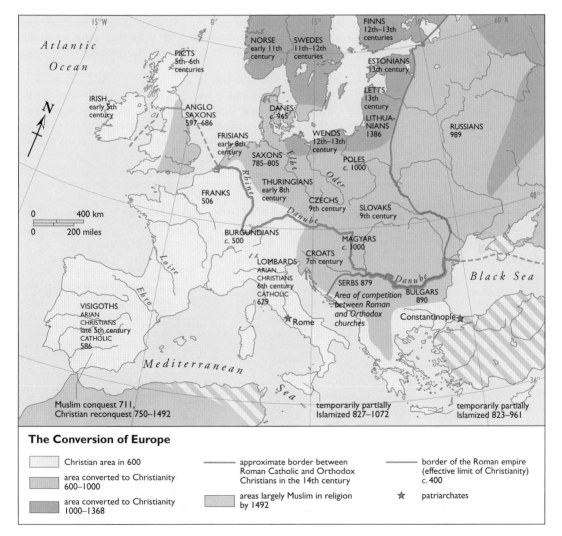

The Conversion of Europe

Christian area in 600

area converted to Christianity 600–1000

area converted to Christianity 1000–1368

approximate border between Roman Catholic and Orthodox Christians in the 14th century

areas largely Muslim in religion by 1492

border of the Roman empire (effective limit of Christianity) c. 400

★ patriarchates

The Arab Conquests

The rise of Islam as a world religion dates from the period of Arab expansionism in the century following the death of Muhammad in 632. By the middle of the 8th century, the Arabian empire stretched from the Indus river in central Asia to the Iberian Peninsula.

"Know that every Muslim is the brother of another Muslim. All are equal. Nobody is superior to another except through piety and good deeds. "

The Five Pillars of Islam

Islam served as the overriding unifying cultural factor among the various ethnic groups living on the Arabian Peninsula. Based on certain truths revealed by God to his prophet Muhammad, the religion of Islam is strictly monotheistic and stems from the Judeo-Christian tradition. God's revelations to Muhammad were written down in the Qur'an, the most important Islamic scriptural text, and a group of followers centred around Muhammad, born around 570 in Mecca (in modern Saudi Arabia), began to adhere to the principles set down by the prophet. Muhammad's popularity grew, but the new religion was left without an obvious leader on his death in 632.

A power struggle ensued, but under Abu Bakr, Muhammad's father-in-law and his first successor, or 'caliph', those Arabs previously sceptical of the prophet's teachings came to accept the Muslim way of life and this unity was cemented through a successful campaign to extend Arab territories. Both urban and nomadic Arabs joined together into a highly effective military force before

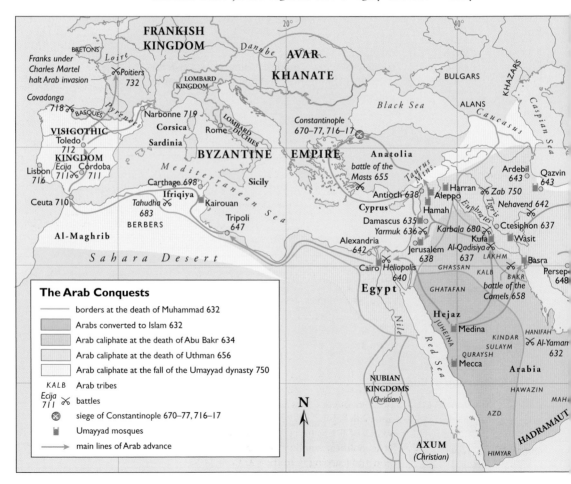

The Arab Conquests

— borders at the death of Muhammad 632

Arabs converted to Islam 632

Arab caliphate at the death of Abu Bakr 634

Arab caliphate at the death of Uthman 656

Arab caliphate at the fall of the Umayyad dynasty 750

KALB Arab tribes

Ecija 711 ⚔ battles

⊛ siege of Constantinople 670–77, 716–17

🕌 Umayyad mosques

→ main lines of Arab advance

which several ancient empires would fall and whose territories would threaten the existence of the Greco-Roman heritage as preserved in the remains of the Roman empire.

Initial conquests were closest to home, and here the Arabs were aided by the financially and militarily debilitating conflict between the Sassanians and the Byzantines. With no chance of alliance and bad shortages of manpower, both powers were unable to stop the newly united Arabs. Roman imperial concerns in Syria and the Middle East fell rapidly during the 630s; Egypt and Rome's other holdings in North Africa went in the next decade. In 651, the Sassanians, successors to the ancient Persians, were forced to place their lands in the hands of Muhammad's followers. In 711 the Arabs entered the Iberian Peninsula, and in the following years all but the Asturias on the north coast of modern Spain capitulated.

The spread of Islam went hand in hand with the Arab conquests. By the end of the Middle Ages, various Muslim empires and caliphates controlled most of Africa north of the Sahara as well as Africa's east coast as far as Kilwa (an island off the coast of modern Tanzania), most of Central Asia to the western borders of modern China, and parts of East Asia. Over half of India and much of the Byzantine empire also had large Islamic populations.

Islamic Culture

Like Hellenistic culture before it, Islamic culture provided important unifying links between what were formerly distinct, and often antagonistic, ethnic groups. Where possible the Arabs took control through relatively non-violent means and the fact that forcible conversion was not practised meant that they were resisted less fiercely in certain areas. In particular, Christian members of the Monophysite churches (adherents of the doctrine that Christ has one nature, part human, part divine) in Syria and North Africa could perhaps be understood as having opted for Islamic political control over enforced conversion to orthodox Christianity. On the whole, the Arabs and their new converts, brought a civilizing influence, political stability and relative prosperity to many of the areas they conquered. Their presence in Europe and other former Roman territories allowed the preservation of a number of ancient advances in science, medicine and philosophy, as well as the survival of important works of literature at a time when Europeans had little political stability and less interest in education and learning than their Arab neighbours.

The magnificent Umayyad Mosque in Damascus, Syria is the oldest monumental mosque in existence. A Roman temple dedicated to Jupiter and later, after the spread of Christianity, a cathedral once stood on this site. After the Arab conquest in 635, Muslims and Christians agreed to partition the church and for the next 70 years performed their respective rituals side by side. In 705 the structure began to be fully converted into the mosque that is seen today.

The Carolingian Empire

The Franks, a barbarian tribe whose kingdom was located in northern Gaul, became the next great European empire after the end of Roman power. Charlemagne, claimed as a hero both by the French and the Germans, extended Frankish territory to include parts of Italy and northeastern Spain, and he and his followers spread their own version of Roman ideals and values across Christian Europe.

"Charles went to Rome, to restore the affairs of the Church ... he received the titles of Emperor and Augustus. He asserted he would not have set foot in the Church [that] day ... if he had known what the Pope was planning to do."

Einhard, *Life of the Emperor Charles*

As Roman power in Gaul weakened, several of the larger barbarian tribes, including the Visigoths and the Burgundians, appear to have operated expansionist policies. It was, however, the Franks, generally popular with their subjects, and early converts to orthodox Christianity, who gained dominance. The Merovingian dynasty, the first important Frankish royal house, took its name from Merovech, grandfather of Clovis I who ascended the throne in 481. Under the Merovingians Frankish territory expanded to include all of Gaul save the Visigothic lands in the southeast corner. Succession problems were to bring about the downfall of the Merovingians as they operated a strict division of inheritance among all legitimate male heirs. This tradition, while ensuring equality within each successive generation, also generally guaranteed dynastic infighting upon the death of each Frankish king or prince. In time these royals became figureheads, with the real power held by the elected office of mayor of the palace. Under Pepin III, who became mayor of the palace in 741, the title of king, as well as the duties and power, was finally seized by these elected officials and the Merovingian dynasty came to an end.

Charlemagne

When Pepin III died in 768, his kingdom was divided between his sons Carloman and Charles. On Carloman's death in 771, Frankish territory was again united under a single ruler. Charles the Great, or Charlemagne, was a wise and forward-looking ruler, but the fact that fate, in removing his brother and thus uniting the Franks, played an important role in Charlemagne's success, ought not to be overlooked. Under Charlemagne Frankish domination was extended from the Iberian city of Barcelona through Aquitaine and down into the Italian kingdom of Lombardy. To the east, the Franks took over the Saxon kingdom and gained a foothold in the former Roman province of Pannonia. Geographical hegemony was coupled with efforts to spread orthodox Christianity, both among the Moorish population in Spain and the Arian Christian tribes (such as the Burgundians). Missionaries were also sent to some of the remaining pagan areas of Europe. Classical ideals of values, education and visual culture were also championed by the enlightened king of the Franks; indeed his reign stimulated a reintroduction of Greco-Roman culture which has been referred to as the Carolingian Renaissance. In 800, Charlemagne was recognized by the papacy as a successor of a kind to the leaders of ancient Rome, and was accordingly crowned emperor on Christmas Day of that year. His title, in time becoming Holy Roman Emperor, would be preserved through generations of German kings.

On Charlemagne's death in 814, the Carolingian empire passed to his only surviving son, Louis the Pious.

The Carolingian gatehouse of the Lorsch monastery, also known as the Königshalle, in Germany. Its architectural style reflects Carolingian preoccupations with Roman building practices. Lorsch was one of the medieval centres of learning.

The Carolingian Empire

- Frankish kingdom at the election of Pepin III, 741
- Frankish gains under Pepin III 741–68
- gains under Charlemagne (768–814)
- Byzantine territory
- ★ major royal palaces
- ○ major monastic centres
- ✪ major archbishoprics
- ★ patriarchate
- ✕ major battles

Louis is remembered primarily for his legal and religious reforms and for his attempts to centralize government throughout the many nations under his sovereignty. Three of Louis' sons survived him and on his death in 840 the empire was divided between them. Under the treaty of Verdun (843) each of the three brothers accepted a portion of Louis' empire. It was then that the centralized power so painstakingly accrued by Charlemagne and Louis began to weaken. For much of the next century further decentralization occurred, culminating in the emergence of French and German political divisions so important in the high and later Middle Ages.

Early Medieval Britain and Ireland

Just as Roman control of Britain evaporated during the 5th century, the Angles and Saxons, invading tribes from continental Europe, swept across southern and eastern Britain forcing the Celtic tribes to retreat to the north and west. Before 800, when the Vikings began to pose a serious threat, the basic demarcations which would result in the creation of England, Scotland, Ireland and Wales were cemented.

"In that same year, after cities had been burned and people slaughtered, Alfred, king of the Anglo-Saxons, honourably made [London] habitable again. And all the Angles and Saxons ... who were not under the rule of the Danes, voluntarily turned to the king and placed themselves under his rule. "

Asser, *Life of Alfred*

Small territories run by local warlords and kings were the norm throughout Britain in the early Middle Ages, with the Picts concentrated in northern Scotland, the Gaelic peoples in Ireland and western Scotland, the Britons in eastern Britain, including Wales and Cornwall, and the newer German tribes in small kingdoms throughout the south and east of Britain.

Christianity arrived in Britain with the Roman missionary team led by Augustine, Archbishop of Canterbury and later saint. In 597 they converted Kent; expeditions to other English kingdoms met with limited success, although the East Angles and the West Saxons had embraced the Roman church by the mid-7th century. Parts of Ireland had been converted during the 5th century and, while the Romans worked to convert Britain from their base in Kent, Irish missionaries set about spreading their brand of Christianity, known as the Celtic rite, across Ireland, Scotland and Northumbria. With its emphasis on isolation and asceticism, Celtic Christianity pressed ever closer to the southern kingdoms loyal to Rome, with Celtic missionaries entering Mercia and Essex after 653. For a while both rites coexisted without conflict, but divergent practices, such as different methods to calculate the date of Easter, made a clash inevitable. At the synod of Whitby (664) delegations from each tradition agreed to unite under Rome; most Celtic Christians capitulated, although strongholds of Celtic Christianity survived in Ireland, Scotland and Wales into the 11th and 12th centuries.

Political Unity

The beginnings of political unification in the British Isles also dates from this period. In Scotland and Ireland, which had never been under Roman control, the ancient kingdoms largely continued. The most powerful kings, including the rulers of the Pictish kingdom of Fortriu and the Uí Néill dynasty in Ireland, expanded their territories by forcing neighbouring warlords to submit to their authority. The ancient Britons controlled three areas: Wales, Cornwall and much of southwestern Scotland. Both Wales and Clydeside grew in power, managing to avoid conquest until the 11th and 12th centuries respectively. In Cornwall pressure from the Anglo-Saxon kingdom of Wessex forced its fall during the 8th and 9th centuries. It was the more powerful Anglo-Saxon kingdoms that made the greatest territorial gains; continuous westward expansion resulted in Northumbria controlling most of northern England and southern Scotland, Mercia the English Midlands, and Wessex all of the southwest. By the mid-10th century, Wessex had succeeded in uniting most of southern England and the western Midlands under one centralized authority; the city of London was already the most important political center for the burgeoning English nation. Much of the kingdom of Mercia had been absorbed into the Wessex-run conglomerate, and the kingdom of Northumbria was also greatly reduced in size. Northumbria, however, had not yielded its territory to the West Saxons; Northumbrian lands in the west had fallen to a new and devastating group of settlers. The Vikings had arrived in the British Isles.

The fortress at Dumbarton Rock on the Clyde river in Scotland was at the centre of the Kingdom of the Britons. It fell to Olaf, the Norse king of Dublin, in 870.

Early Medieval Britain and Ireland

- ▪▪ ▪▪▪ Mercia *c.* 730
- ⊬⊬⊬ course of Offa's Dyke
- *c.*780 date of submission to Mercia
- ★ major royal centre
- Gaelic territory *c.* 800
- ✙ major church
- Pictish territory *c.* 800
- ⚔ battle
- British territory *c.* 800
- ◦ other important site
- Anglo-Saxon territory *c.* 800

N

Atlantic Ocean

North Sea

Irish Sea

English Channel

Birsay
Orkney
Caithness
Udal
Applecross
Moray
Craig Phadrig
Mortlach
Deer
Pictland
Forteviot
Brechin
Dunnottar
Dunkeld
Nechtansmere 685
Northumbrian expansion halted by the Picts
Dunollie
Scone
Iona
Dundurn
St. Andrews
Dál Riata
Dunblane
Fortriu
Dunadd
Govan
Dunbar
Dumbarton
Glasgow
Edinburgh
Coldingham
Britons of Strathclyde
Melrose
Lindisfarne
Abercorn
Yeavering
Bamburgh
Bernicia
Mote of Mark
Hexham
Jarrow
Whithorn
Carlisle
Monkwearmouth
Rowley Burn 633
Whitby
Ailech
Derry
Ulaid
Bangor
NORTHUMBRIA
Northern Uí Néill
Airgialla
Nendrum
Ripon
Deira
Inishmurray
Clogher
Downpatrick
Winwaed 654
York
Armagh
Manaw
Connacht
Southern Uí Néill
Kells
Monasterboice
Hatfield 633
Cruachu
Knowth
Irish Sea
Deganwy
LINDSEY *c.*780
Ardagh
Tara
Lagore
822
Lincoln
Clonmacnoise
Durrow
Naas
Aberffraw
Chester 616
Kilfenora
Kildare
Gwynedd
Oswestry 641
Crowland
EAST ANGLIA *c.*730
Inishcaltra
Glendalough
Powys *c.*822
Lichfield
Leicester
Ely
Laigin
Rendlesham
Cashel
Ferns
Ceredigion
Llanbadarn Fawr
Builth
Tamworth
MERCIA
Ipswich
Ardfert
Munster
Worcester
Northampton
West Saxon victory ended Mercian dominance
Lismore
Hereford
Inisfallen
Cork
Garryduff
Brycheiniog
ESSEX *c.*730
Skellig Michael
Garranes
St David's
Llangorse Crannog
Dyfed
Gloucester
St. Albans
Barking
Glywysing
Llandaff
Ellendun 825
London
Llanilltud Fawr
Dinas Powys
Bath
Rochester
according to legend, the birthplace of King Arthur
WESSEX *c.*733–52
Winchester
Canterbury
SUSSEX *c.*760
Tintagel
Sherborne 786–802
Hamwih
KENT *c.*764–76 785–95 807–25
Exeter
Wimborne
Dumnonia

0 ___ 200 km
0 ___ 100 miles

The Vikings

The Vikings, fearsome warriors from Scandinavia, swept across Europe during the 9th and 10th centuries. After c. 865 most Viking raids were simply attempts by various warlords to gain wealth and prestige rather than territory.

(Norse settlement occupied c.1000–1020)

> *"The Norsemen plundered ... Frisia and razed the town of Dordrecht.... The Norsemen returned to their own lands, their ships filled with great booty, both possessions and slaves. "*
>
> Annals of Xanten, 846

'Viking' is a general term applied to any of the loosely-bound clans originating in present-day Norway, Denmark and Sweden. Scholars are divided on the initial causes of Viking expansionism; overpopulation, lack of arable lands and political upheavals have all been suggested. Whatever the reasons, Viking raids grew more frequent from the late-8th century and they had abated, almost as inexplicably, by the mid-11th century.

Pattern of Viking Settlement

Geographically, the pattern of Viking raids corresponds roughly to the home territory of each of the main groups. The Swedish Vikings swept south into eastern Europe, opening trade routes down to the Black Sea and as far west as the Caspian Sea; the tribe known as the Rus lent its name to the emerging Slavic state of Russia. The Norwegian clans, known as Norsemen, headed west to northern Britain and then to the Faroe Islands, Iceland, Greenland and Ireland where they established the first urban settlements. Danish control of eastern England, known as the Danelaw, and further gains in the south meant that in the years following 1000 the Danish king Cnut briefly ruled an empire which included Denmark, Norway and England.

Perhaps the key to the success of the Vikings was their ability to acculturate in the areas they settled. They intermarried and adopted local cultures with ease, although this was not due to a lack of any meaningful cultural heritage of their own. Northern England and Scotland still abound with Scandinavian place names and surnames, obvious signs that the invaders did not simply relinquish their own culture in favour of British customs. Normandy became a Frankish royal duchy under the Viking leader Rollo in 912, and here again one finds the same ability to adopt the native culture. Feudal relationships in Normandy, for instance, were often simpler than elsewhere in France; the Normans had adopted the Frankish custom and utilized it far more effectively than its original proponents. Even after their acceptance into the Frankish political system, the Normans maintained their characteristic desire to expand and colonize. It is through the Norman mother of Edward the Confessor, king of England, that William, Duke of Normandy claimed the English throne in 1066.

Permanent Viking settlement was limited to parts of Britain and Ireland, Iceland, Greenland and Normandy. Viking artefacts, mostly portable objects like jewellery, have been found along their routes in and around Europe. Further proof of the extent of their travels is revealed in the coins found in some Viking burials indicating trade with, or theft from, a host of kingdoms throughout Europe. Evidence of Viking activity in northern Newfoundland, perhaps the Vinland mentioned in ancient Viking lore, has been carbon-dated to the years around 1000, making the Vikings the first Europeans to visit the Americas.

An etched Viking picture stone in Gotland, Scandinavia. The etchings, which date to the late-8th century, include a Viking ship. Hundreds of these stones were erected as memorials to the dead between the 6th and 10th centuries.

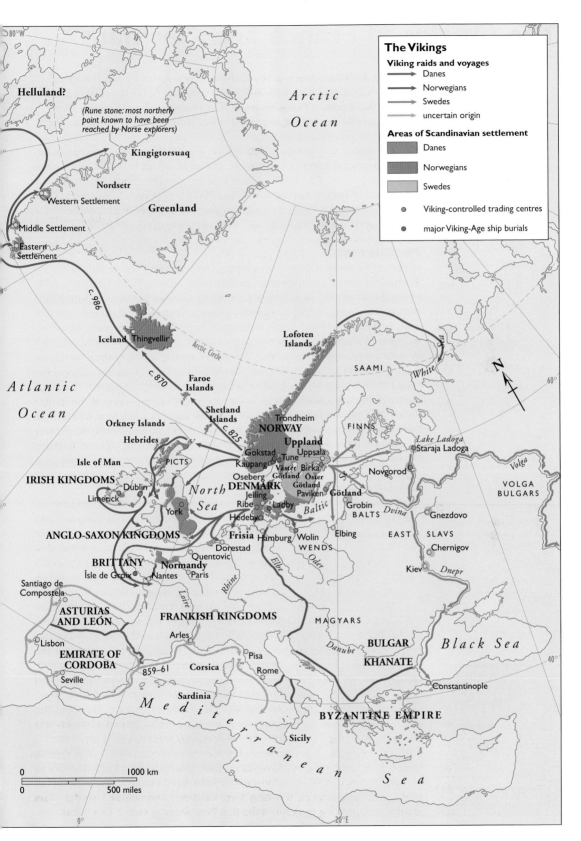

The Vikings

Viking raids and voyages

Danes
Norwegians
Swedes
uncertain origin

Areas of Scandinavian settlement

Danes
Norwegians
Swedes

Viking-controlled trading centres

major Viking-Age ship burials

Helluland?

(Rune stone: most northerly point known to have been reached by Norse explorers)

Arctic

Ocean

Kingigtorsuaq

Nordsetr

Western Settlement

Greenland

Middle Settlement

Eastern Settlement

c. 986

Iceland Thingvellir

Arctic Circle

c. 870

Faroe Islands

Atlantic

Ocean

Shetland Islands

c. 825

Orkney Islands

Hebrides

Isle of Man

PICTS

IRISH KINGDOMS

Dublin

Limerick

York

North Sea

ANGLO-SAXON KINGDOMS

BRITTANY

Île de Groix

Normandy

Nantes Paris

Santiago de Compostela

ASTURIAS AND LEÓN

Lisbon

EMIRATE OF CORDOBA

Seville

Arles

859–61

Corsica

Pisa

Rome

Sardinia

Mediterranean Sea

Sicily

Lofoten Islands

SAAMI

White Sea

FINNS

Trondheim

NORWAY

Uppland

Gokstad

Tune Uppsala

Kaupang

Väster Birka

Oseberg Götland Öster

DENMARK Götland

Jelling Paviken **Götland**

Ribe Ladby

Hedeby Grobin

BALTS

Frisia Hamburg Wolin Elbing

Dorestad WENDS

Quentovic

Oder

Elbe

Rhine

Loire

FRANKISH KINGDOMS

MAGYARS

Danube

BULGAR KHANATE

Lake Ladoga
Staraja Ladoga

Novgorod

Volga

VOLGA BULGARS

Gnezdovo

Dvina

EAST SLAVS

Chernigov

Kiev *Dnepr*

Black Sea

Constantinople

BYZANTINE EMPIRE

N

0   1000 km

0   500 miles

31

The Origins of France and Germany

After the failed division of the Carolingian empire by the Treaty of Verdun in 843, the authority of Charlemagne's heirs was eroded. By the late 9th century five kingdoms had emerged; two of these, West and East Francia, would become France and Germany respectively.

The Carolingian empire, save for Provence, was briefly reunited under Charles the Fat, great-grandson of Charlemagne, but on his death in 887 dynastic struggles again erupted. Carolingian control of the new kingdoms was nominally maintained in France, Germany, Italy and Provence; Burgundy was ruled from 888 by the heirs of Rudolf I, a member of the Welf family from Bavaria. Provence and Italy, despite Carolingian royalty, were really controlled by local noblemen.

The Capetians

In France, the western half of the empire, Charlemagne's descendants were not generally up to the job. Some, like Louis IV, ruled quite well, implementing basic political centralization and reigning with little internal conflict, but by the late-10th century real power had shifted to regional rulers. The most influential of these was probably Hugh Capet, duke of the Franks, who contrived to have himself elected king by the French nobility. Hugh Capet, plagued during his reign by attempts to topple him, instituted a major Capetian tradition: the formal nomination of his eldest son, Robert, as his successor while Hugh himself was still alive. This began a pattern of public relations for which the Capetian dynasty is famous. Revival of Carolingian traditions of complex coronation and burial rites and of the royal touch as a cure for disease added to the family's popularity. Real gains in territory and wealth were made possible by recovering the ancient feudal rights due the French crown. The Capetians turned their office into one of the most influential in medieval Europe and they ruled France until 1328.

Late Carolingian Germany

The Carolingian position in Germany remained strong through the 9th century, especially during the long reign of Louis the German (died 876). Son of Louis the Pious and a grandson of Charlemagne, Louis was given the kingdom of East Francia in 825 and, from his base in Bavaria, was able to extend his rule over most of the Germanic peoples. Louis fostered a new sense of national identity through his support of German culture. At the end of his reign Germany looked set to follow a course similar to France, wherein political centralization and cultural similarities would result in a unified nation state. Several factors intervened, however, notably military conflicts against the Vikings, Slavs and Magyars. While on one level protecting East Francia from these invaders served to unite the Germans, it also meant that limited attention was paid to the machinery of large-scale government. Also, in the late-9th century a succession of weak Carolingian rulers allowed the regional nobility to gain power. What later emerged was a group of principalities, duchies and counties each with a local power base. However, after Henry I of Sax-

0 — 400 km
0 — 200 miles

N

Aachen

KINGDOM OF CHARLES II THE BALD

KINGDOM OF LOUIS THE GERMAN

Tributary areas

KINGDOM OF LOTHAR I

Rome

PATRIMONY OF ST PETER

Treaty of Verdun 843

ony's election to the German throne in 919 and the birth of the new Ottonian dynasty, so-named for Henry's successors, Otto I, Otto II and Otto III, great strides towards German political unification were made. Yet, regional power struggles forced the Ottonians to rely heavily on the ecclesiastical hierarchy of the Roman church to rule their subjects. This dependency would result in a conflict between Church and State which still reverberates today.

Origins of France and Germany

— borders in 888

Frankish Kingdoms in 888

Muslim territory

areas of Scandinavian settlement

✠ principal archbishoprics and bishoprics

→ Viking raids, 9th century

→ Magyar raids, 10th century

NORSE

DANES

North Sea

Hedeby

PRUSSIANS

Kolobrzeg
POMERANIANS

ABODRITES

IRISH KINGDOMS

Dublin

KINGDOM OF YORK

York

WELSH KINGDOMS

Danelaw

KINGDOM OF WESSEX

London

Founded 962 by Otto I as a base for operations against the Slavs

Bremen

Saxony

Magdeburg

POLES

SORBS

Oder

✠ Cologne

EAST FRANCIA (GERMANY)

Lorraine

Mainz

Prague

BOHEMIANS

Traditional place for the coronations of the kings of France

Rhine

Normandy

Reims

Trier

Franconia

Danube

MORAVIANS

Vienna

48°

Seine

Paris

BRITTANY

Sens

Swabia

Lechfeld 955

Bavaria

Salzburg

MAGYARS
c.896

Tours

Loire

Nantes

Bourges

BURGUNDY

Otto I routs the largest Magyar army to invade Germany

Atlantic Ocean

WEST FRANCIA (FRANCE)

Lyon

Aquileia

CROATS

Sava

Bordeaux

Vienne

Embrun

Pavia

Milan

Venice

Po

Genoa

Ravenna

NAVARRE

Auch

PROVENCE

Arles

Aix-en-Provence

Pisa

KINGDOM OF ITALY

SERBS

ASTURIAS AND LEÓN

Narbonne

Marseille

Pyrenees

Rhône

ARAGON

Ebro

Barcelona

Corsica

Rome

Patrimony of St Peter

Bari

Salerno

Duchy of Benevento

BYZANTINE EMPIRE

EMIRATE OF CORDOBA

Sardinia

Balearic Islands

Mediterranean Sea

Sicily

0
400 km

0
200 miles

60°N

N

33

Part 1I: The Revival of Europe

At the turn of the millennium, Europe was dominated by a collection of military aristocracies which controlled local populations by the use or threat of force. Political power resided in the ownership of land, and kingship, although recognized everywhere as the normative form of government, was subject to severe local constraints. The English and Frankish kingdoms were vulnerable to destructive raids by the Arabs from the south and the Vikings from the north and west.

Public authority in most of Europe was determined by accommodation and con- sensus among the most powerful landowners. Although written law codes existed, the powers of law and order were wielded by the locally powerful rather than by appointees of royal authority. The low level of literacy outside the monasteries meant that government in most of Europe, with the exception of England, remained unsophisticated. Lack of security, poor communications and a lack of economic stimulus contributed to a static level of education and learn- ing. Since the 5th century, western European culture had evolved as a synthesis of what could be remembered of the classical heritage coupled with Germanic aristocratic and royal traditions. The Church, although providing the dominant culture of belief, had little autonomy and no unified leadership.

Western Europe survived on a subsistence economy that managed to feed a static population of around 20 million. Huge areas of Europe were still unset- tled: large areas of undrained marshland and intractable forests or wildernesses dominated much of the landscape. It was a mainly rural society. There were few towns, and most of those would by modern standards count as villages. Com- mercial activity was mainly based on local markets where barter and exchange was normal. Only small amounts of coinage circulated; even kings derived most of their revenues from services or tributes in kind rather than cash.

Growth of Europe

By 1300, all this had changed unrecognizably. Now it was Europe that posed the threat to frontiers that had been pushed further east and south than ever before. New towns had been founded in huge numbers across Europe, representing the internal colonization of previously uninhabited regions as well as outward expansion. Trade routes crisscrossed the continent, and a new urban middle class with economic purchasing power pushed up demand for luxury goods from the East. The wealthiest among Europe's aristocracy, particularly in the Mediterranean, enjoyed an ostentatious consumption beyond the imaginings of the feudal lords of 300 years earlier. Europe was now shaped by a small number of kingdoms run by centralized bureaucracies based on literate administrative and accounting systems and supported by sophisticated and articulate theories of royal power. Among these monarchies was a papal government with a com- plex bureaucracy whose purpose was to channel the regional government of the Church towards its centre in Rome.

A revolution had transformed Europe's cultural life. The university, a creation of the 12th and 13th centuries, maintained and regulated a system of higher edu- cation that produced graduates trained for the practical arts of government and theologians whose work advanced the philosophical underpinnings of Christ- ian culture. The rediscovery of classical learning that made this possible also resulted in an explosion of vernacular literature that reflected the growing com- plexity of medieval society. Around *c.* 1000, it was still possible to characterize society according to the three categories of those who fought, those who prayed and those who worked the land. By 1300, whole new categories, such as professional lawyers, clerks, students, teachers and merchants, had emerged.

These changes make this 300-year era the most dynamic of all medieval periods. Yet it is easy to exaggerate the parlous state of European society in c. 1000. Not all of western Europe was in a state of anarchy or collapse. The German monarchy provided a model of strong kingship centred on ritual and ideal. Emperor Otto III, who married the Byzantine Princess Theophano, established a sophisticated court in which Byzantine cultural influences were prominent. The defeat of the Magyars by his grandfather, Otto I, in 955, not only assured security from the east, but symbolized the return of an imperial rule that looked back to Charlemagne. England, despite undergoing a Danish invasion that removed the native ruling dynasty from power in 1014, remained a stable and prosperous society with well-established laws and governmental procedures. The election to the papal throne of Gerbert, Archbishop of Ravenna, in 999 presaged the development of a powerful centralized papacy later in the 11th century. A noted scholar and teacher before becoming Pope Silvester II, Gerbert upheld moral reforms within the Church that were to be championed by the Gregorian reform movement from 1049 onwards.

Uniting the Spiritual and the Secular

Signs of revival are also discernible elsewhere. Attempts to limit the effects of destructive private warfare were begun by bishops in Aquitaine and Burgundy in 989. Through the creation of 'peace leagues' to which prominent regional landowners were invited to swear membership, the bishops hoped to create coalitions of secular and spiritual power to police an endemically violent society. Although the 'Peace and Truce of God' movement, as it was known, may have been minimal in curbing violence, both the impetus to achieve such reform and the methods employed mark an important stage in the development of European society. The breakdown in the social and political order was treated by contemporaries as a moral issue. The significance of the Peace Movement lies in its harnessing of the spiritual authority conferred by relics, oaths and presiding bishops with the military power of the aristocracy. The relationship between these two forces was mutually beneficial. Bishops and monasteries secured protection from arbitrary acts of violence or theft against church lands. At the same time, for those knightly families that valued it, a close relationship with a local monastery brought a degree of legitimacy to their claims to lordship.

The conditions of disorder in the early 11th century that gave rise to the Peace Movement exposed the live wires of the power dynamics in western society. The Church as a collection of institutions was bound into relationships with local landowners. This was partly because bishops and abbots were themselves typically members of the aristocracy, and sometimes even trained warriors. Moreover, parish and collegiate churches and monasteries were usually the property of the lay families that had founded them, that continued to appoint clergy and abbots to them, and expected to enjoy a share in their prosperity. Patterns and

The Abbey Church of Saint-Etienne in Caen, Normandy. The church was founded under the patronage of William the Conqueror in 1064 and he was buried there in 1087. William commissioned the church after the pope lifted the ban on his proposed marriage to Matilda of Flanders. The church was intended to symbolize a new harmony between Church and government. It is also known as the Men's Abbey as devotion there was intended for males only.

expressions of religious devotion also maintained these links between the aristocracy and the Church. Piety was usually expressed through the cultural practice of gift-giving to local churches or monasteries. Gifts not only enhanced the donor's standing and prestige, they also held the promise of tangible benefits in the form of intervention or political favour from the bishop. More profoundly, however, they were a guarantee that a surrogate penance would be done on behalf of the donor and his family by the religious community to which a donation had been made. A contractual obligation was thus created between spiritual power and secular wealth, and this interdependence between the lay nobility and the Church set the tone for the ways in which medieval society would organize itself for centuries to come.

Papal Reform Movement

At the highest political level as well as at the level of local communities, the relationship between spiritual and secular authority dominated Europe in the 11th century. It was shaken profoundly, however, by a revolution within the Church. From mid-century onwards, a group of reforming monks and clergy wrested control of the papacy from Roman aristocratic families. That this was initially accomplished through the initiative of the German emperor Henry III indicates the value placed on the prestige of the papal office. In political theory the relationship between papal and imperial power symbolized the Christian Roman empire of the age of Constantine. By 1075, however, the papal reform programme had sidelined the imperial role in the running of the Church. Pope Gregory VII, summing up a generation of reforming ideology, undermined traditional political theory when he declared that popes had authority not only to withhold the rite of imperial coronation from an emperor, but even to depose kings. The German imperial response to this challenge, from 1080 onwards, resulted in a theory of absolute kingship based on biblical authority upon which European rulers would continue to call beyond the Middle Ages.

Many of the most prominent reformers, including Popes Gregory VII (1073–85) and Urban II (1088–99), were themselves monks, and their reform ideals – the freedom of the Church from lay interference, celibacy for the clergy and the prohibition of payments for church offices – were in essence monastic ideals. The reform of the Church hierarchy was promoted by the most powerful monastic institution in Europe – the Burgundian monastery of Cluny and its daughter-houses. Cluny had been founded in 910 on the principle of freedom from lay authority and dependence on the papacy rather than on either the bishop or the founding family. In 1059, the papacy freed itself in a similar fashion with a decree establishing free elections to papal office by the college of cardinals.

It would be wrong to assume that the papal reform movement represented simply a high-minded elite within the Church. The popularity of Cluniac monasticism among the laity, and the respect in which it was held in society at large, are testimony to the wider desire for moral reforms within the Church. In most of Europe, the parish clergy was perceived as inadequate. As marriage among clergy was commonplace, parish priests often inherited the office from their fathers. Education among the clergy was poor, so Christian instruction of the laity was scant. In rural society, the village priest was probably little different in manner of life, background or outlook from most of the peasantry. During the 11th century, a grass-roots revivalism seems to have demanded improvement in the Church's performance. The willingness of lay landowners to enter partnerships with monasteries, to join peace leagues, and to undertake pilgrimages, are all symptoms of this trend. In some Italian towns, such as Florence and Milan, there were riots against bishops perceived to be enemies of reform.

One consequence of 11th-century reform idealism was conflict between the two powers whose mutual relationship had been regarded until the 1070s as a reflection of divine order in the universe: the papacy and the empire. The Investiture Conflict, as it has become known, upset this relationship by promoting the idea of a papal monarchy as the head of Christian society. Periodically, even after the settlement of the conflict in 1122, discord broke out again between popes and emperors.

Power Struggle

At root for much of the period was the question of the extent of each power's authority. In the 13th century, however, the long-running dispute between the papacy and the Hohenstaufen emperor became a crude struggle for power in Italy. Although the ideal of papal monarchy was maintained by the papacy throughout the 12th and 13th centuries, it made little headway in practice against the developing secular monarchies, particularly of France and England. While kings paid lip service to the principle of free elections to bishoprics, in practice they could not permit such vital positions to be filled without playing some role in the process.

The political unity of England created in the 10th century by the dominance of Wessex over its neighbours was reinforced by the Norman Conquest of 1066. The combination of an efficient Anglo-Saxon governmental system and an authoritarian Norman military aristocracy resulted in strong monarchical rule based on consensus between kings and landowners. When this consensus broke down, as for example in the civil war during the reign of King Stephen

Exterior view of the Palazzo Pubblico in Siena, Italy. Siena's importance as a civic centre began in the 12th century when a self-governing commune replaced the aristocratic government. The commune gradually increased its territory as the neighbouring feudal nobles submitted to the growing urban power. Florence was Siena's great political and artistic rival in the 13th century when construction of the Palazzo Pubblico began. The tall bell-tower, or Torre del Mangia, is the tallest tower in the city and once rang the time and announced curfews and council meetings.

(1135-54), the great magnates enjoyed almost unbridled licence to rule over their territories without recourse to royal will. The return of firm government under Henry II (1154-89) and his Angevin heirs, Richard I (1189-99) and John (1199-1216), was achieved by the use of law to fix land inheritance. Angevin government marked the rise of law over custom in English political culture. However, when the crown ran into political difficulties, as John was to discover, the barons could use the same process to set limits to royal authority. An arbitrary style of kingship highly dependent on the king's own personality gave way in 13th-century England to an enforced consensus between the crown and baronial representation. The crown's ability to generate money from its landowning subjects depended on keeping such consensus; by 1300, however, the barons in Parliament were demanding a voice in how such money should be spent.

A combination of dynastic accident and aggressive expansion from the mid-11th to the mid-12th century resulted in the dominance of the Norman-Angevin dynasty over most of France and England. Under the shadow of this dominance, however, the French monarchy also began to assert strong centralized rule in the 12th century. Beginning from the small base of the Ile-de-France around Paris and Orleans, the Capetian dynasty expanded its influence over the independent duchies and counties of France, and under Philip II Augustus (1180-1220) took on and defeated the Angevins. This feat was accomplished largely through the exercise of strict feudal principles. Beginning within the small but agriculturally prosperous royal demesne land, the French kings succeeded in enforcing obedience based on formal recognition of their authority as head of the feudal hierarchy; in this way, they were able to intervene in and put an end to private warfare between their vassals. The expulsion of the Angevin John from his hereditary possessions of Normandy and Anjou in 1204 was the result of the application of the same principles on a larger scale.

The tribune of Sainte-Chapelle in Paris, France. Louis IX built the chapel to house the holy relics, including the Crown of Thorns, he purchased at an exorbitant price from the Byzantine emperor in 1239. The cost of the relics exceeded the cost of the chapel itself. Located within the Palais de Justice complex, the chapel was a religious and political symbol of the king's dual function, as both temporal and spiritual leader. The Sainte-Chapelle is famous for its magnificent stained-glass windows and bold Gothic architecture.

Government in France, England, the papacy and Sicily became increasingly sophisticated in the 13th century through the employment of university graduates in the royal bureaucracies. The replacement of custom by written statute made arbitrary rule by kings more difficult, although without necessarily weakening royal authority; indeed, the formalization of consensus granted by parliaments in France and England may have strengthened it. By 1300, the national monarchies of England and France had replaced the Holy Roman empire as the dominant force in European politics.

The intellectual revival of the 12th century was centred on the cathedral schools of northern France. The application of the secular arts, particularly logic, to the study of the Bible, produced a new scholarly synthesis. This came to fruition in the creation of a new academic corporation of students and teaching masters: the university. For the first time, a uniform syllabus of study came into being, governed by the award of degrees. The huge expansion of higher education in the 12th and 13th centuries was only possible because of the increased availability of leisure and manpower among the class of lesser landowners or urban bourgeoisie from which most students came. As government became more ordered and conditions throughout Europe more secure, sons who were not required to inherit family land could take advantage of the possibility of travel to wander from one centre of learning to another.

The dissemination of learning in its turn affected the provision of pastoral care within the Church, as the complex theology of the schools was adapted for use in preaching and confessional manuals. The revival of learning was only one aspect of a more widespread cultural revival. Alongside improvements in the study and use of Latin came the development of vernacular literatures, particularly in Provençal, northern French and German. Centred in courts rather than in monasteries, these literary forms catered for the aristocracy, reflected their sense of common identity and promoted their ideals of chivalric behaviour.

Monastic Reform

From the late 11th century, monasticism itself adapted to new forms of spirituality. Poverty and withdrawal from society were the ideals of a new generation of reformers, among whom the most influential were the Cistercians. Claiming to return to the 'pure' monasticism of the Rule of St. Benedict, the Cistercians' insistence on manual labour rather than relying on income from tenancies and tithes resulted in an agricultural economy based on the direct cultivation of land. By c. 1200, however, this system had, probably unintentionally, made many reforming monasteries wealthy. A new wave of reform, exemplified by the creation of the mendicant orders, was partly a response to the perceived failure of monasticism to live up to its own reforming agenda. The mendicants, or friars,

The Old Synagogue in Prague in the Czech Republic is the oldest functioning synagogue in Europe. The Jews suffered bouts of persecution and expulsion throughout the Middle Ages, notably during the Crusades. Built in about 1270, the Old Synagogue has survived pogroms, fires and redevelopment in the course of its long history.

differed in one important respect from monks: their mission was one of instruction rather than contemplation, and they thus became a feature of the urban rather than rural landscape. The need for instruction, chiefly in the form of preaching, was necessitated by the failure of the parochial church before the 13th century to provide adequate pastoral care. Most clergy were uneducated and therefore unable to preach. One consequence was the spread of heretical beliefs. Some of these derived from dissatisfaction with the pace of reform and were wholly orthodox in origin, but the most prevalent, Catharism, rejected Catholicism altogether and offered an alternative set of beliefs.

The Church regarded heretics in much the same way as the Jews: as people who refused to conform to the self-evident truth of Christianity. Medieval theologians thought that the continued existence of the Jews was necessary as a perpetual reminder of their error. They could not control popular sentiment, however, and from c. 1100 onwards, intolerance towards the Jews grew; there were periodic massacres in England, France and Germany in the 12th century, often linked with crusading fervour.

The period between 1000 and 1300 saw dramatic progress in human achievement in Europe: in culture, learning and the arts, in understanding the environment and in a more nuanced spirituality, in law and the craft of government, in technology and the agricultural economy. The other side of these achievements, however, was a more marked chauvinism within European society. For the majority, Europe in 1300 was securer and more prosperous than it had been in 1000. Its increasingly self-confident and articulate bureaucracies, however, made it less tolerant of diversity and of those regarded as deviant.

The Papacy

"Our Lord Jesus Christ summoned us to kingship; he did not summon you to priesthood .... You have even laid hands on me, though I am anointed to rule, which is against the tradition of the holy Fathers who assert that I can be judged only by God. "

Henry IV, Letter to Pope Gregory VII

The reforming popes of the later 11th and early 12th centuries initiated profound changes within the Roman Church. Their reforms led to the development of a new ideology of leadership which fostered the rise of the papacy as a powerful political force.

For most of the early Middle Ages, popes had little authority outside Rome. The Church was largely run by bishops at a regional level. This suited most secular rulers, who relied on their bishops to administer regional government since they, unlike most secular lords, tended to be well-educated, and could not, because of their celibacy, found dynasties. The German kings, who also served as Holy Roman emperors, used the church hierarchy to counter the influence of the regional nobility. In time, the investiture ceremony, wherein a bishop was presented with the symbols of his office, came to include an oath of allegiance to his secular overlord. By the 11th century, the ceremony, and often the selection of the candidate himself, had fallen to imperial or royal representatives.

The second half of the 11th century saw the election of popes from non-Roman families. More importantly, many of the reforming popes were informed by monastic ideals, rather than the traditions of the secular clergy. The first reformer, Leo IX, tried to rid the Church of practices that compromised its moral authority, including clerical marriage, simony (the buying or selling of clerical offices) and lay investiture of bishops. Subsequent reforming popes secured freedom of papal election, so as to reduce imperial influence over the office.

Ideological Conflict

Reform first led to conflict in 1075, when the archbishopric of Milan fell vacant, and the local clergy, with papal backing, elected a reformer. Formerly a protégé of Leo IX, Pope Gregory VII was committed to reform and convinced of the supremacy of the papacy. Emperor Henry IV had his own candidate invested by Lombard bishops loyal to him. Henry backed down, but the confrontation escalated again resulting in Henry deposing the Pope on 1 January, 1076, only to find himself in turn excommunicated by Gregory. Henry IV could not afford to lose control of such a strategically important centre as Milan, but if Gregory allowed northern Italy to fall under the sway of the emperor, Rome would effectively be cut off from its transalpine allies. Just as military conflict seemed unavoidable, Henry met Gregory at Canossa to seek absolution. He received it on 28 January, 1077, after three days of petitioning. This episode set an important precedent, strengthening the new political role of the Church and weakening the already precarious influence of the emperor over his Italian territories and his German vassals. Constitutionally, the most significant aspect of the dispute was Gregory's insistence that the Pope had the authority to depose kings.

Authority was one thing, however, and power another. Despite the Pope's inability to enact the deposition, the conflict continued to rage. It was settled only with an uneasy compromise by the Concordat of Worms (1122) between Pope Calixtus II and Emperor Henry V. The Church would appoint and invest bishops, who would swear an oath of allegiance to the emperor, either as part of the investiture ceremony or, preferably, prior to it. Seen by many historians at least in part as a personality clash between two strong-minded men, Pope Gregory VII and Henry IV, over a specific set of circumstances, the Investiture Conflict led tangentially both to the development of a new political ideology for the papacy as well as a codification of the concept of kingship, and, in turn, of the temporal sovereignty of the developing nation state.

Emperor Henry IV (1050–1106) is depicted in this 12th-century illuminated manuscript asking Countess Matilda of Tuscany to intervene in his dispute with Pope Gregory VII in 1077.

The Papacy: Reform and Conflict

— major political divisions c.1100

Holy Roman empire c.1100

Byzantine empire

areas of Norman control

other Christian areas

✛ major archbishoprics

★ patriarchate

■ reforming councils (date)
(1095)

▣ origins of reforming popes
1 Leo IX, 1049–54
2 Victor II, 1055–7
3 Stephen IX, 1057–8
4 Nicholas II, 1058–61
5 Alexander II, 1061–73
6 Gregory VII, 1073–85
7 Victor III, 1086–7
8 Urban II, 1088–99

▢ important members of the *Fideles sancti Petri*
1 Matilda of Tuscany
2 Raymond IV of St-Gilles, Count of Toulouse
3 William Tête-Hardi, Count of Burgundy
4 Robert, Count of Flanders
5 Welf IV, Duke of Bavaria
6 Hugh of Lusignan

The Holy Roman Empire

The elected kings of Germany, by tradition also Holy Roman emperors, needed to consolidate power and wealth to secure dynastic supremacy. Under Frederick I Barbarossa and his grandson, Frederick II, the extent and political power of the Holy Roman empire was stretched to breaking point.

"I made your chieftain my vassal and put you under my power; it is I who am lawful ruler of Rome. Let he who is able snatch the club from the hand of Hercules … The hand of the German has not yet lost its strength!"

Frederick Barbarossa to the people of Rome, from Otto of Freising, *The Two Cities*

When Frederick Barbarossa, son of a Hohenstaufen father and a Welf mother, was elected king in 1152, two of Germany's most powerful noble families were united. Despite this, Frederick possessed neither the security enjoyed by hereditary rulers, nor the financial base to defend his position within Germany. With this in mind, Frederick, also Holy Roman emperor elect, began to assert his imperial rights within Italy. Direct rule over the whole empire would result in financial dominance and allow Frederick to assert his notional supremacy over other European kings. Initially he attempted to subdue Lombardy by appointing his own episcopal candidates, but the papacy, much strengthened since the Investiture Conflict, continued to fight secular interference.

Frederick I

Frederick was crowned emperor in 1155 only after having agreed not to ally himself with the Normans or other enemies of the papacy, a promise which he kept until he learned that the Pope had made peace with the Normans. Now Frederick began in earnest to assert his imperial rights over Lombardy. He installed legates in each city and exacted taxes in exchange for feudal services owed him. Frederick's policies were popular neither with his Italian subjects nor with the papacy, which was worried about mounting imperial control over Lombardy. When Frederick backed the election of Pope Victor IV in 1159, the cardinals elected Alexander III who excommunicated Frederick. The emperor was quickly abandoned by his allies. After initial success in war against the Lombard towns, Frederick was defeated at Legnano in 1176 and forced to recognize Alexander as pope. Although Frederick ultimately failed to gain control over his empire, he is remembered for his centralizing rule over his German territories. Frederick I also at times displayed singular diplomatic skills and the unexpected result of one of his alliances was the inheritance of the Holy Roman empire and the Kingdom of Sicily by his grandson, Frederick II.

The marriage between Frederick Barbarossa's son, Henry, and Constance, aunt of King William II of Sicily, became momentous when William died suddenly in 1189, leaving his throne to Constance. In 1197 Frederick, still a boy, became king of the Germans and of Sicily. The geographical spread of his realms, with many regions politically unstable, and the distrust of a papacy now surrounded by Hohenstaufen lands, made Frederick's position difficult. To assert control over his territories, Frederick issued laws to regularize the machinery of governance. The best known of these, the *Liber augustalis* (1231), attempted to institute a single legal system throughout Frederick's Italian lands. As king of Sicily, Frederick was seen by popes as their vassal; as emperor, he insisted on his rights as an equal. Under Popes Gregory IX (1227–41) and Innocent IV (1243–54), relations between the Church and Frederick disintegrated into open warfare. Innocent had the emperor, already twice excommunicated, convicted of perjury and heresy and deposed in 1245. Frederick countered by declaring the Pope incompetent and questioning his right to depose an emperor. Accusations, most unfounded, continued on both sides until Frederick died in 1250. His lands were again divided and his debates with the papacy left unresolved.

In this late-10th century illumination, the German king and emperor, Otto III, is enthroned between two sets of representatives, the spiritual on one side and the worldly on the other.

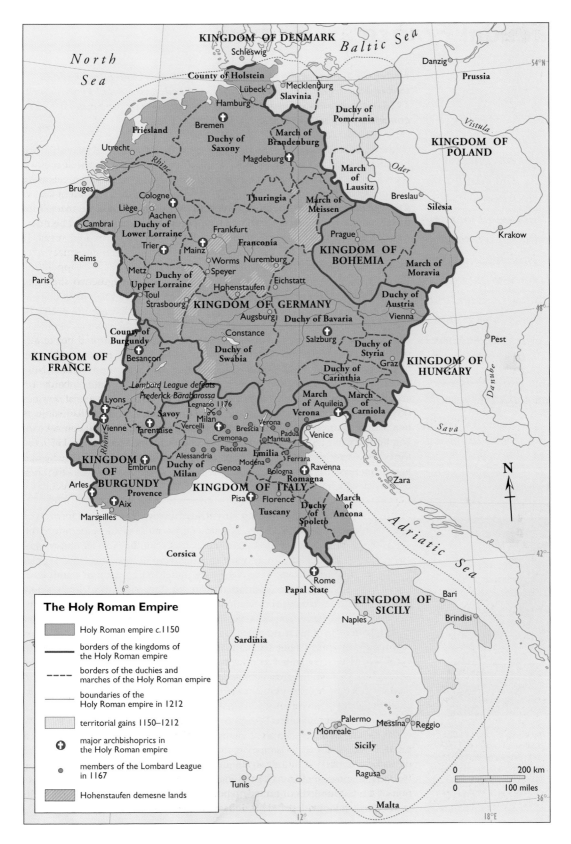

KINGDOM OF DENMARK
Baltic Sea
North Sea
Schleswig
County of Holstein
Danzig
Prussia
Lübeck
Mecklenburg
Slavinia
Hamburg
Duchy of
Pomerania
KINGDOM OF POLAND
Bremen
Friesland
Duchy of
Saxony
March of
Brandenburg
Vistula
Utrecht
Magdeburg
March of Lausitz
Oder
Bruges
Cologne
Thuringia
March of Meissen
Breslau
Silesia
Liège
Aachen
Cambrai
Duchy of
Lower Lorraine
Frankfurt
Prague
KINGDOM OF BOHEMIA
March of Moravia
Krakow
Reims
Trier
Mainz
Franconia
Worms
Nuremburg
Metz
Speyer
Duchy of
Upper Lorraine
Eichstatt
Duchy of
Austria
Paris
Toul
Hohenstaufen
KINGDOM OF GERMANY
Strasbourg
Vienna
Augsburg
Duchy of Bavaria
County of
Burgundy
Constance
KINGDOM OF FRANCE
Besançon
Duchy of
Swabia
Salzburg
Duchy of
Styria
Pest
Graz
KINGDOM OF HUNGARY
Duchy of
Carinthia
Danube
*Lombard League defeats
Frederick Barabarossa*
March
of Aquileia
March of Carniola
Legnano 1176
Verona
Lyons
Savoy
Milan
Verona
Sava
Vienne
Tarentaise
Vercelli
Brescia
Padua
Venice
Cremona
Mantua
Piacenza
Emilia
KINGDOM OF BURGUNDY
Embrun
Alessandria
Modena
Ferrara
Zara
Duchy of
Milan
Genoa
Bologna
Ravenna
Romagna
Adriatic Sea
Arles
Provence
KINGDOM OF ITALY
Pisa
Florence
March of Ancona
Aix
Tuscany
Duchy
of
Spoleto
Marseilles
N
Corsica
Rome
Papal State
Bari
KINGDOM OF SICILY
Naples
Brindisi
Sardinia
Palermo
Messina
Reggio
Monreale
Sicily
Ragusa
Tunis
Malta

The Holy Roman Empire

Holy Roman empire c.1150

borders of the kingdoms of
the Holy Roman empire

borders of the duchies and
marches of the Holy Roman empire

boundaries of the
Holy Roman empire in 1212

territorial gains 1150–1212

✚ major archbishoprics in
the Holy Roman empire

• members of the Lombard League
in 1167

Hohenstaufen demesne lands

0   200 km
0   100 miles

54°N
48°
42°
36°
6°
12°
18°E

Feudal France

Under the Capetian kings, France emerged as a centrally governed and tightly organized political power. The dynasty ruled France until 1328 and contributed greatly to the development of the modern concept of the nation state.

"Louis [VI] disinherited some of the knights in the castle and seized their goods; others he condemned to long imprisonment ... Through this great victory, won with God's help against the expectations of his rivals, he augmented the crown's revenue."

Suger, *The Deeds of Louis the Fat*

Of the 15 Capetian kings, all but two succeeded their fathers, and their ability to produce healthy and long-lived male heirs greatly contributed to the success of the Capetian dynasty. Undisputed succession and long reigns, both relatively uncommon in medieval Europe, provided France with a potential economic and social stability undreamt of elsewhere. However, even a smooth succession of long-lived rulers would not have helped a royal house lacking in political and strategic ingenuity.

Using Feudal Rights

Hugh Capet (938–996), the founder of the line, was elected in 987 to the French throne, at this time a relatively insignificant position with a small royal domain and no real wealth or power base. Hugh's reign did little to raise the profile of the French throne, but he is remembered for instituting the practice of crowning his son as his heir during his own lifetime, an attempt to ensure a straightforward succession. Hugh's son, Robert II the Pious, began the process of strengthening the royal position. He commissioned a biography emphasizing his piety and good works and promoted the Royal Touch, a Carolingian tradition alleging that physical contact with the person of the king could cure scrofula (a skin disease). Perhaps his most important contribution, however, was his use of feudal rights to increase royal land holdings. Many ancient charters were revived and Robert was quick to claim any fines due him as chief overlord or any territories left vacant or with disputed heirs. This strategic use of feudal ties would in time increase the royal domain and secure royal influence over those French territories which remained independent.

The tombs of John and Blanche, children of Louis IX (1214–70) and Marguerite of Provence at the Saint-Denis Basilica in Paris, France. Many French monarchs and nearly all the Capetian royals are buried at Saint-Denis.

Strengthening Royal Authority

Robert's lead was followed by most of his successors; the rights of the king to collect fees and fines, to administer justice and to appoint candidates to ecclesiastical and secular positions were rigorously upheld. The revival of Carolingian traditions continued with the introduction of increasingly elaborate coronation and burial ceremonies, both designed to raise the public profile of the king himself and of the sanctity of his royal office.

Under Louis VI (the Fat), the position of the French king magnified in power and prestige. Louis initiated a campaign to bring to heel unruly vassals, regardless of their power and wealth. Louis' tactics resulted in a compact centrally-governed, if still small, state within which royal authority was undisputed. Respect for the monarch increased dramatically when, as king of France, he alone managed to muster a united army to prevent the Holy Roman Emperor Henry V from invading France. The same use of feudal rights by a Capetian king, albeit on a much larger scale, was implemented by Philip II Augustus, grandson of Louis VI, who in 1204 managed through the exaction of feudal penalties to claim a significant portion of the French lands held by the English kings.

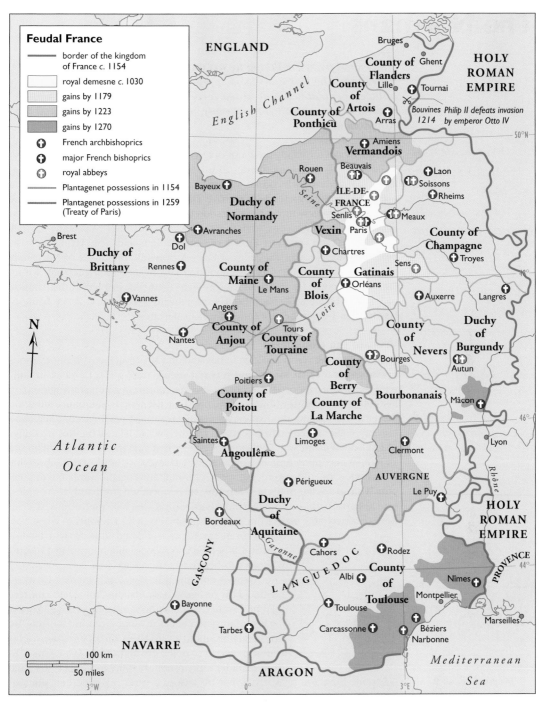

Feudal France

— border of the kingdom
   of France c. 1154

▢ royal demesne c. 1030

▢ gains by 1179

▢ gains by 1223

▢ gains by 1270

✠ French archbishoprics

✠ major French bishoprics

✠ royal abbeys

— Plantagenet possessions in 1154

— Plantagenet possessions in 1259
   (Treaty of Paris)

ENGLAND

Bruges

County of Flanders   Ghent

HOLY ROMAN EMPIRE

County of Artois   Lille   Tournai

County of Ponthieu   Arras

Bouvines Philip II defeats invasion
1214   by emperor Otto IV

50°N

Amiens

Vermandois

Rouen   Beauvais   Laon

Bayeux   Soissons

Rheims

ÎLE-DE-FRANCE

Duchy of Normandy   Senlis   Meaux

Avranches   Vexin   Paris

Brest   Chartres   County of Champagne

Dol   Troyes

Duchy of Brittany   Rennes   Sens

County of Maine   County of Gatinais

Le Mans   of   Orléans   Auxerre   Langres

Blois

Vannes   Angers   Tours   County of Nevers   Duchy of Burgundy

Nantes   County of Anjou   County of Touraine   Bourges   Autun

County of Berry

Poitiers   Bourbonanais   Mâcon

County of Poitou   County of La Marche

Atlantic Ocean   Saintes   Limoges   Clermont   Lyon

Angoulême

Périgueux   AUVERGNE

Duchy   Le Puy

of   HOLY ROMAN EMPIRE

Bordeaux   Aquitaine

Cahors   Rodez   PROVENCE

GASCONY   Albi   County of   Nîmes

LANGUEDOC   Toulouse   Montpellier

Bayonne   Toulouse   Béziers   Marseilles

Tarbes   Carcassonne   Narbonne

NAVARRE   Mediterranean Sea

N

ARAGON

0   100 km

0   50 miles

3°W   0°   3°E

Louis IX, canonized in 1297, was the best-loved Capetian king. His long reign (1226–70) and his saintly lifestyle ensured him popularity and underscored the Capetian claim of the divine right to rule. Louis died on crusade in Tunis in 1270 and immediately became the focus of great popular veneration. The direct line of the Capetians ended in 1328 with the death of Charles IV the Fair, a great-grandson of Louis IX. The throne passed to a side line of the family, the House of Valois, but every future king of France would descend from the Capetian line.

The Normans

Descended from the Viking Rollo (died 932), the first duke of Normandy, the Normans were renowned for their expansionist policies, centralized power and ferocity in battle. By the 12th century, the Normans controlled Normandy, much of the British Isles and the Kingdom of Sicily.

"They are a people accustomed to war, so that they can scarcely live without it; they charge the enemy fiercely, but whenever force itself is not enough, they are just as prepared to use some stratagem or to corrupt with bribes. "

William of Malmesbury, *Ecclesiastical History*

The duchy of Normandy grew out of territory along the River Seine granted to Rollo by the French king Charles III the Simple in 912. The Norsemen, or Normans, converted early on to Christianity, adopted feudal land tenure and mastered Frankish methods of warfare. The restlessness which often led to the colonization of new territories may stem from the result of feudal customs that disinherited younger sons. Robert and Roger Guiscard left Normandy for Italy around 1050 and conquered much of southern Italy and Sicily, laying the basis for the future Norman Kingdom of Sicily. Meanwhile the dukes of Normandy soon earned the respect of neighbouring barons and their territory within France expanded. The death of King Edward the Confessor led to the invasion of England by Duke William the Bastard, Edward's cousin and at the battle of Hastings on 14 October 1066, the Normans defeated the English.

William the Conqueror

Duke William was crowned king of England on Christmas Day 1066, but various uprisings meant that his control was not secure until 1071. He dealt brutally with those who opposed him, but he also saw advantages in many Anglo-Saxon institutions, such as the shire system and the legal system, and improved upon these by introducing the Exchequer and itinerant justices. To secure England's borders, William invaded first Scotland and then Wales. Like all the Norman kings of England, William saw England as a colony that needed to run efficiently to allow him maximum time in Normandy. The Domesday Book (1086) represents an overview of land tenure and wealth throughout England, probably to compute William's assets in his new territory. He bequeathed Normandy to his eldest son, Robert Curthose, and England to his second son, William II Rufus. William Rufus exacted large taxes from his English subjects in his attempts to wrest Normandy from his brother and did little to win English approval. When he was killed while hunting in 1100, his younger brother, Henry, succeeded him.

Henry I continued to develop centralized government and the justice system, claiming to be less arbitrary than his brother, while at the same time making it easier for his treasury to collect revenue from his subjects. He defended his right to award lands and titles to men of his choosing, and in so doing created a class of 'new men' to rival the older, more established noble families. His reign

This detail from the Bayeux Tapestry shows the Normans fighting Harold's men at the battle of Hastings. Harold Godwinson had seized the English throne after Edward's death in 1066. Most historians agree that the embroidery was commissioned by Bishop Odo, William the Conqueror's half-brother, soon after the battle.

was quite long and prosperous, but his lack of a surviving male heir plunged England into civil war. His daughter Matilda claimed the throne on Henry's death in 1135 with the backing of many of Henry's 'new men'. Matilda's second husband, Geoffrey of Anjou, was, however, less popular among the Norman subjects owing to his Angevin connections. Stephen of Blois, like Matilda a grandchild of William I, was the rival claimant. Years of violent conflict followed Henry's death, with Stephen emerging as king only in 1148. Stephen died in 1154 and his kingdom passed into the hands of Henry II, Matilda's son and the first Angevin king of England.

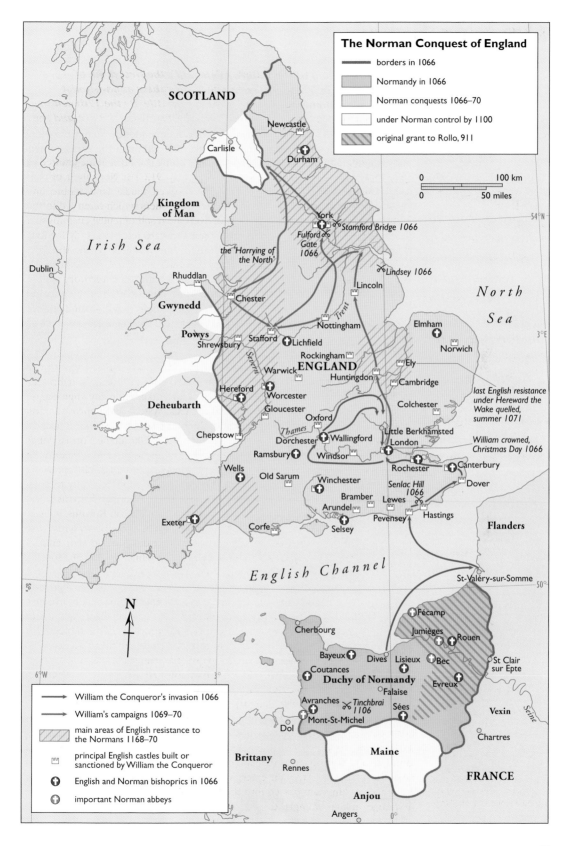

The Norman Conquest of England

- borders in 1066
- Normandy in 1066
- Norman conquests 1066–70
- under Norman control by 1100
- original grant to Rollo, 911

0   100 km
0   50 miles

SCOTLAND

Newcastle
Carlisle
Durham

Kingdom of Man

York — Stamford Bridge 1066
Fulford Gate 1066
the 'Harrying of the North'
Lindsey 1066

Irish Sea

Dublin

Rhuddlan
Chester
Gwynedd
Lincoln

North Sea

Powys
Shrewsbury
Stafford
Nottingham
Lichfield
Rockingham
Warwick
ENGLAND
Huntingdon

Elmham
Norwich

Ely

Cambridge

last English resistance under Hereward the Wake quelled, summer 1071

Deheubarth
Hereford
Worcester
Gloucester
Oxford
Chepstow
Dorchester
Wallingford
Ramsbury
Windsor

Colchester

London
Little Berkhamstead

William crowned, Christmas Day 1066

Wells
Old Sarum
Winchester
Bramber
Arundel
Lewes
Pevensey

Rochester
Canterbury
Dover

Senlac Hill 1066
Hastings

Exeter
Corfe
Selsey

Flanders

English Channel

St-Valéry-sur-Somme

N

Cherbourg
Fécamp
Jumièges
Rouen

Bayeux
Dives
Lisieux
Bec
St Clair sur Epte

Coutances
Duchy of Normandy
Falaise
Evreux

Avranches — Tinchbrai 1106
Sées
Vexin

Dol
Mont-St-Michel

Maine

Brittany
Rennes

Chartres

FRANCE

Anjou
Angers

- William the Conqueror's invasion 1066
- William's campaigns 1069–70
- main areas of English resistance to the Normans 1168–70
- principal English castles built or sanctioned by William the Conqueror
- English and Norman bishoprics in 1066
- important Norman abbeys

Norman Sicily

The southern half of the Italian peninsula during the 11th century was an arena in which different ethnic and political groupings competed for dominance.

The Lombard lords of the Campania wanted independence from a Byzantine protectorate whose grip was steadily weakening; although the areas immediately south of Rome were Catholic, Apulia and Calabria had largely Greek-

"[Roger II] made efforts to administer justice ... on the grounds that it was particularly necessary for a newly established realm, and to exercise the options of peace and war, with the result that he omitted nothing that virtue requires, and had no king or prince as his equal in his lifetime."

Hugo Falcandus,
History of the Tyrants of Sicily
(Manchester University Press, 1998)

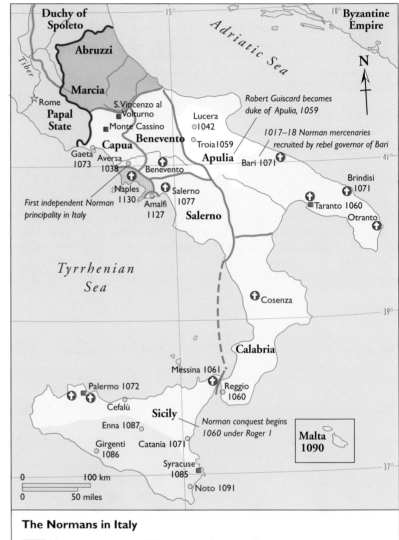

The Normans in Italy

☐	Norman acquisition to c. 1059
☐	Norman acquisition to c. 1085
☐	Norman acquisition to c. 1091
☐	Norman acquisition to c. 1130
☐	Norman acquisition to c. 1154
▬	border of Byzantine empire c. 1000

☆	patriarchate
✚	archbishoprics
■	Catholic monasteries
■	Orthodox monasteries
—	border of the Kingdom of Sicily c. 1154
1060	date captured by Normans

speaking populations and Greek religious institutions, while the island of Sicily was divided between Greeks and Arabs. Norman warriors first entered this arena in the 1030s as mercenary forces fighting at times for the Lombards and

at times for the Byzantines. By 1042, however, William Ironarm, a member of the de Hauteville family of Normandy, had been recognized as count of Apulia, and Norman clans increasingly began to see southern Italy in terms of permanent settlement. William's brother Robert Guiscard, who became count of Apulia in 1059, extended Norman rule over Naples, Salerno and Calabria, and having thrown the Byzantines out of their last stronghold of Bari in 1071, tried in the 1080s to invade the Byzantine empire. His brother Roger, meanwhile, embarked in the 1060s on the invasion of Sicily, which became another Nor-

man county. Guiscard used a combination of military muscle and diplomatic skill to create an alliance with the papacy: at the treaty of Melfi in 1059 Norman rights to rule over conquered lands were granted in return for recognition of papal overlordship. This relationship was to prove troubled over the next 200 years, but it worked to the Normans' advantage by protecting the legitimacy of their rule against the counter claims of the German emperors. This was particularly important after 1130, when Count Roger II of Sicily was recognized as king over all Norman lands in Italy in return for his support for the papal candidate Anacletus II. Roger successfully defended his new kingdom against invasion from the papacy and Emperor Lothar II.

The white marble pillars inlaid with polychrome decoration at Monreale Cathedral in Sicily reveal Arab influence on the island despite Norman rule. The splendid mosaics at Monreale are a mixture of Arab, Byzantine and Norman styles that illustrate the best of the Christian and Muslim worlds of the 12th century.

Byzantine Style

Roger (1130–54) and his successors William I ('the Bad' 1154–66) and II ('the Good' 1166–89) deployed their wealth and new status to create an image of kingship to emulate their rivals. They adopted Byzantine imperial robes and insignia, and the glittering mosaics of the royally endowed churches at Palermo, Monreale and Cefalù were based on Byzantine models and worked by artists trained in Byzantine style and methods. They were buried in porphyry tombs in imitation of the popes. The Arab cultural heritage of Sicily was also flaunted, both in Norman court culture and in government, where the financial administration was run in Arabic and using Arab bureaucrats. Notwithstanding their vassalage to the papacy, the Norman kings promoted an ideology of independence of authority, promoted by the mosaic cycle at Monreale showing the coronation of the kings directly by Christ. This independence of the papacy was also shown in the Norman kings' tendency to favour Greek monasteries as opposed to the new Cistercian Order. However, the famed 'multiculturalism' of the Norman kings can be exaggerated. The Muslim population of Sicily waned from the late 12th century, and Greeks and Arabs mostly remained peasants.

The Norman kings' involvement on an international stage can be seen in the planned invasion of Egypt by William II in 1174 and his sack of Thessalonika in 1182. However, his death without heirs left the kingdom to his sister Constance and her husband, the Holy Roman Emperor Henry VI. In opposition to German domination, Tancred of Lecce, a grandson of Roger II, had himself crowned king in 1190, but his death in 1194 brought the Norman dynasty to an end.

The coronation of Roger II as king of Sicily (1130), from a mosaic in the church of La Martorana at Palermo. Roger's Byzantine robes and coronation by Christ himself reflect both his cosmopolitan outlook and his hostility towards the papacy.

The Angevin Empire

The Angevin empire, which at its height included more of France than did the Capetian kingdom, numbered among its rulers the most beloved and hated of the English kings.

"Indeed [Henry II] does not, like some other kings, loiter in his palace, but travels throughout the provinces to examine what everyone is up to, judging powerfully those whom he has set up to judge others. "

Peter of Blois,
Letter 66 (1177)

Henry II of England was crowned at Westminster on 19 December 1154; son of Matilda, daughter of Henry I, Henry succeeded his cousin Stephen of Blois. Henry II is remembered as the 'Father of English Law' for his attempts to regularize the Crown's use of feudal law as an instrument of income and control, a move which found great favour among the English barons. Henry's passionate nature, however, could at times betray a certain rashness of action, such as when four of his knights acted on what they believed were his wishes and murdered the Archbishop of Canterbury Thomas Becket in 1170 in Canterbury Cathedral.

Henry's choice of queen is noteworthy in terms of the advance of the Angevin cause. Eleanor, Duchess of Aquitaine and Countess of Poitiers, had previously been married to Louis VII of France, a weak king and Eleanor's equal in neither intellect nor passion. The marriage failed to produce a male heir and Louis divorced his fiery wife only to look on in horror as she quickly allied herself with Henry II. This marriage proved extremely successful; England now controlled more of France than did the Capetians, and the couple produced eight children, with four sons and three daughters surviving infancy.

Richard the Lionheart

His eldest son having predeceased him, Henry died in July 1189 and his crown fell to his son Richard, the legendary lion-hearted king. Richard had a reputation for foolhardy personal courage combined with astute leadership in war. Always more at home in his ancestral possessions, Richard rarely visited England, but this was because the centralized machinery of government in England required his presence infrequently. He died of a wound in 1199, having freely used his feudal ties to exact crippling payments from his English subjects.

As Richard had produced no heirs, John, the youngest son of Henry II and Eleanor of Aquitaine, inherited the throne. Convinced that Arthur of Brittany, son of his deceased brother Geoffrey, would attempt to claim the English throne from him, John contrived to have himself recognized as a vassal of the French king in his capacity as Duke of Normandy. With this title secure, John had little to fear from Arthur, although he had him murdered in 1202, just in case. Soon after his oath of homage to King Philip II Augustus of France, John abducted a noblewoman, Isabelle of Angoulême, and forced her to marry him. His Poitevin vassal Hugh IX of Lusignan, claiming to be betrothed to Isabelle, followed feudal protocol by taking his complaint against John to John's overlord, Philip II of France. The French king called John to Paris to explain his actions, and when John failed to appear, declared his possessions in France forfeit to the French Crown; shortly afterwards a French army invaded Normandy. The loss of Normandy and the other northern French territories was particularly painful as these were the historical power base of the English kings. To fund his battles against the French, John was forced to return to the arbitrary feudal practices of his great-grandfather Henry I, exacting heavy taxes and fines in England. By 1215 his barons had had enough; a chastened King John was forced to put his seal to Magna Carta, measures designed not to weaken the monarchy, but rather to protect the baronage from the random whims of the king.

The Tomb of Eleanor of Aquitaine (c.1122–1204), queen of France and later England, in Fontevrault Abbey in France. The tombs of two Plantagenet kings, Henry II and Richard I, lie alongside that of Eleanor.

N

Hebrides
(to NORWAY)

0 ——— 200 km
0 ——— 100 miles

SCOTLAND

Perth ○   ○ St Andrews

Edinburgh   ○ Berwick

Harbottle   ○ Warkworth
Wark   Newcastle
Carlisle   ○ Durham
Appleby   Richmond
Brough
Thirsk
Lancaster   ○ York
Malzeard
Pontefract   Axholme
Stockport   Conisbrough
Rhuddlan   Peak Duffield   Lincoln
Chester   Nottingham
Tutbury   Mountsorrel
Shrewsbury   Leicester   Norwich
Coventry   Bungay
Bridgnorth   Framlingham
Cardigan   Builth   Warwick   Huntingdon
Hereford   Northampton   Orford
St David's   Oxford   Colchester
Carmarthen Gloucester   London
Pembroke   Rochester
Bristol   Windsor   Dover
Salisbury   Canterbury
Southampton   Winchester
Exeter ○   Chichester   Boulogne

North Sea

KINGDOM OF MAN

Irish Sea

IRELAND
Connacht
Meath
Athlone   Dublin
Leinster
Limerick
Cashel ○
Munster
Cork ○

Carrickfergus
Ulster
Armagh ○

Gwynedd
Powys
Deheubarth

ENGLAND

Flanders

English Channel

Bouvines 1214
Bouvines 1214   Tournai

HOLY ROMAN EMPIRE

Eu
Arques   Amiens
Barfleur   Aumâle   Vermandois
Drincourt   Gournay
Bayeux   Rouen   Vaudreuil   Reims
Caen   Gisors
Évreux   Château-Gaillard
Pontorson   **Normandy**   Paris
Avranches   Argentan   Nonancourt   Champagne
Verneuil
Dol   Alençon   Bellême   Gatinais
Fougères   Mayenne   **Maine** La Ferté-Bernard   Troyes
Brittany   Le Mans
Rennes   Sablé   Vendôme   **FRANCE**
Vannes   Angers   Tours   Blois Chinon
Ancenis   Saumur   Loches   Ste Maure
Nantes   Nivernais
Anjou   Loudun   Bourges
Parthenay   Preuilly   Issoudun
Poitou   La Haye   Burgundy
Vouvant   Poitiers   **Touraine**
La Rochelle   Niort   **Bourbonnais**
Taillebourg   Lusignan
Saintes   Marcillac   La Marche
Pons   Angoulême   Limoges
Chateauneuf-sur-Charente   Limousin   Clermont
Aquitaine   Le Puy
Périgueux   Auvergne
Périgord
Bordeaux

Bay of Biscay

Argenais   Cahors
Agen   Rodez

Gascony
Armagnac   **County of Toulouse**   Nîmes ○
Auch   Toulouse
Bayonne
Béarn   Narbonne
Bigorre
CASTILE
NAVARRE   **ARAGON**

The Angevin Empire

Growth of the Angevin empire

lands inherited by Henry II, 1150–4

lands acquired by Henry's marriage to Eleanor of Aquitaine

lands acquired by conquest or diplomacy

lands acknowledging Henry II as overlord

lands claimed by Henry II

principal castle or stronghold

castle held against Henry II during the rebellion of 1173–4

Collapse of the Angevin empire

campaigns of Philip II and his allies, 1202–4

campaigns of John and his allies, 1214

campaigns of Philip II and his allies, 1214

French territory retained by John in 1214

The Kingdoms of Hungary and Poland

Along with their central European neighbours, Hungary and Poland benefited little and late from the cultural and political advances of western Europe. Alternately coveted as buffers against invasions from Asia and brushed aside as poor relations, both kingdoms struggled to achieve sovereignty at home and recognition abroad.

❝[Following the death of King Stephen] songs played on lutes quickly turned to lamentations all over Hungary. The Hungarians ... mourned him with faithful hearts and great, inconsolable sadness. ❞

Illustrated Chronicle of Mark Kalt concerning the Deeds of the Hungarians, Chapter 70 (between 1358 and 1370)

The Magyars, later known as Hungarians, were invited to settle the Danube basin by the Carolingian emperor Arnulf in 892. Árpád was elected as leader; his dynasty lasted until the death of Andrew III in 1301. Roman Christianity was adopted by Géza I in 975 and Géza was able to marry his son Stephen to a Bavarian princess in his bid to become respected in the West. The reign of King, later Saint, Stephen I was a long and prosperous one which saw the introduction of systems of land tenure, social class structure and bishoprics. Relations with the papacy and various western rulers were established, with care taken to avoid reliance on imperial favour which might threaten Hungary's sovereignty.

For much of the 11th and 12th centuries Hungary was in political turmoil, ruled by a series of largely ineffectual kings with disputed claims to the throne. Despite this, Christianity became firmly rooted and a feudal system, wherein a small nobility oversaw land worked by underclasses, developed. Through dynastic intermarriage connections with the West were cemented, and the Hungarian court became recognized as a centre of high culture, although intellectual and literary life at court would reach its zenith later under King Mattias Corvinus. For much of the later Middle Ages, Hungary was ruled by foreigners, some with tenuous connections to the

The Kingdom of Poland

— borders of Poland under Boleslaw the Brave c.1138

— borders of Polish duchies

▨ Polish territory granted to the Teutonic Knights in 1228

✛ archbishoprics

✛ bishoprics

⛰ seats of Polish princes

➡ Mongol invasion, 1241

Árpád dynasty. Hungary's geographic location caused even greater problems. Mongols from the East invaded in 1241, ravaging the countryside, and, in 1526, the forces of the Ottoman empire began an occupation that would last nearly 200 years.

Unlike Hungary, Poland's borders have changed numerous times since its foundation in the 10th century. Mieszko I, an early member of the Piast dynasty, converted to Christianity in 966 and pledged his allegiance to the Pope rather than to the emperor. Boleslaw I the Brave was crowned as Poland's first king in 1024. He increased the number of Polish bishoprics, further strengthening his connections with the papacy. Two centuries of unrest followed Boleslaw's death in 1025 and only the strong relationship between the Church and Poland remained unchanged. The situation was improving by the 13th century, due in part to increased trade with the rest of Europe. As in Hungary a system of land tenure adapted from western feudalism was put in place, but Polish rulers were stuck in a continual fight for regional supremacy between Poland, Hungary and Bohemia. Late medieval Poland remained locked in a subordinate role within Central Europe, unable to rise above its regional divisions.

The Crown of St. Stephen (c. 975–1038), the first king of Hungary. According to Hungarian tradition, Pope Silvester II sent a magnificent gold jewelled crown to Stephen in recognition of his position as king.

The Kingdom of Hungary

- —— border of Hungary c.1200
- ⧄ Hungarian territorial gains, early 13th century
- ✚ archbishoprics
- ✚ bishoprics
- ◼ royal monasteries
- → Mongol invasion 1240–2

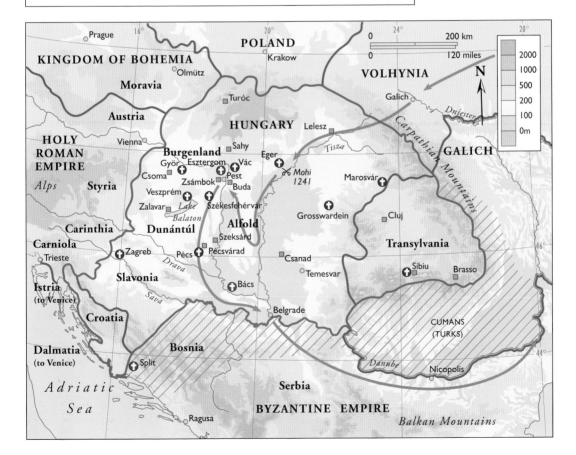

The Medieval Church

The Catholic Church was the single most important institution in medieval Europe. As a mediator between feuding territories and a promoter of learning and the arts, the Church provided a unifying cultural experience for nearly all Europeans. Christianity informed all aspects of medieval life and most people pledged their primary allegiance to God, rather than to any temporal power.

"The archbishops must not neglect to hold annual provincial councils with their bishops. In these they should be inspired by a genuine fear of God in correcting faults and reforming morals, especially the morals of the clergy."

Fourth Lateran Council, Canon 6

Most secular rulers demanded, often rather arbitrarily, payment in the form of military service, rents and taxes from their subjects; in return they provided, equally arbitrarily, justice and protection. The Church, on the other hand, could provide most benefits offered by a secular lord, as well as spiritual solace and the possibility of eternal salvation.

Although never entirely free from corruption or greed, the clergy demanded relatively little from the ordinary Christian: financial support, generally in the form of tithes made up of a fixed portion of one's annual income paid in cash or in kind, regular attendance at Mass and participation in the sacraments. Parish priests accompanied parishioners through every stage of life, baptizing babies, blessing the infirm, burying the dead and absolving sinners. Marriage, previously regarded solely as a legal contract, fell increasingly under the jurisdiction of the Church in the 12th century, and the formal responsibility for education was provided by cathedral schools under episcopal oversight.

Spiritual and Secular Life

For medieval people, nobles and peasants alike, there was no concept of a division between their spiritual and secular lives. Utilizing celebrations within the liturgical year to designate annual secular events such as payment of rents or to mark university terms should be seen not as encroachment by the Church, but as examples of the seamless nature of spiritual and temporal life. On a more mundane level, the physical presence of churches, monasteries and cathedrals – often the only stone buildings in a village or town – lent height, majesty and an otherwise unknown sense of permanence to the landscape. Stained glass, sumptuous vestments and colourful wall paintings each afforded parishioners a glimpse of somewhere immeasurably better and potentially attainable for those who lived according to Christian principles.

Each community had at least one parish staffed by a priest who could administer the sacraments and carry out pastoral duties. Parishes were grouped into dioceses each of which was presided over by a bishop, who in turn frequently reported to an archbishop who held the largest or most important bishopric in the region.

The *Institution of the Crib at Greccio* from the Legend of St. Francis (1297–1300) in the Church of San Francesco in Assisi. To promote worship among ordinary people, Francis had a crib set up in a cave near Greccio, thus starting the tradition of preparing a crib in memory of Christ's birth at Christmas. The fresco is set inside the church, viewed from the presbytery, and as women were not allowed to enter the presbytery, they can be seen looking on from the doorway of the transept.

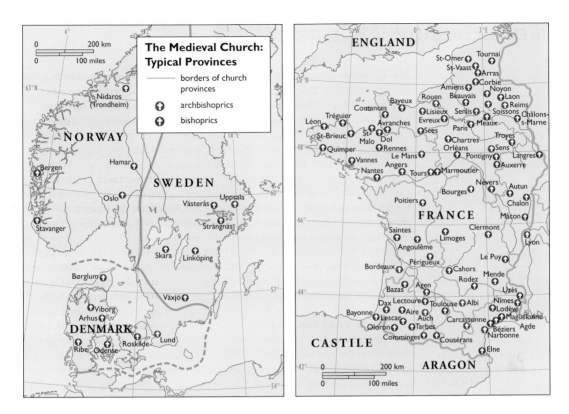

The Medieval Church:
Typical Provinces

— borders of church provinces
☩ archbishoprics
☩ bishoprics

The Pope, himself the bishop of Rome, was at the head of the ecclesiastical hierarchy; his position assumed much greater power and responsibility following the Investiture Conflict of the late 11th and early 12th centuries. Deacons occupied the lowest position within the clergy, serving as unordained helpers to priests and bishops. Cardinals, who staffed the papal curia (the central administration of the Roman Catholic Church), could be deacons, priests or bishops. The title of cardinal was originally an honorary one given only to clergy who held important positions within the city of Rome itself. From the late 9th century, however, popes could only be chosen from among them, and by 1179 the College of Cardinals had secured the right to elect the Pope.

From c. 1000 to 1300 a more international constituency among the cardinals was actively sought by the Church. The success of this arrangement is perhaps best illustrated by the early implementation of the diocesan system in those areas of Europe which had longest resisted Christianity and large-scale political unification, namely Central Europe and the Baltic States. Bishops accustomed to administering large populations and unable to found rival dynasties were acknowledged as necessary to establish control. Unlike the older bishoprics found in most of western Europe, these new dioceses were often large and their incumbents were closely allied to the ruler. The diocesan system allowed careful control over a newly unified population.

Lund Cathedral in southern Sweden is the finest example of Romanesque architecture in the Nordic region. King Cnut (c. 994–1035) founded the city of Lund in 1020 and it later became the political, religious and cultural centre of the whole of Scandinavia.

Benedictine Monasticism

Monasticism was born in the eastern Mediterranean in the period between the 3rd and the 6th centuries. Early monastic practice in Egypt, Syria and Palestine centred on austere forms of self-denial, either in communal (cenobitic) or solitary (anchoritic) settings.

"We are, therefore, about to found a school for the service of the Lord, in which we hope to introduce nothing harsh or burdensome."

Rule of St. Benedict

Monasticism was introduced in the West largely through the writings of John Cassian (*c.* 360–435), formerly a monk in Egypt who founded a community near Marseille in the early 5th century. The monastic tradition which came to dominate in the West was the Rule written in the mid-6th century by Benedict of Nursia. Benedict set up a community at Monte Cassino in Italy based on a moderate form of cenobitic monasticism that emphasized the virtues of stability and obedience to a superior. Prospective Benedictine monks took vows of poverty, obedience and chastity, and after a year's novitiate they were supposed to remain in the community until death. The monastic day was divided into three functions: work, prayer and sleep. The organizing principle, known as the daily offices, was the liturgical observance within the abbey church.

Serving the Lay Community

Benedict envisioned his monasteries as self-sufficient communities supporting themselves through manual labour. However, as Benedict's ideas proved popular in early medieval Europe, monasticism evolved to take on the needs of lay society. Most important of these was the role of the monastery in the penitential system. As many foundation charters of monasteries make clear, powerful laypeople who left bequests to monasteries expected spiritual rewards in return: the prayers of the monks in perpetuity would help to offset the sins committed during life. As the economy of early medieval Europe was based on land holdings rather than currency, most of these bequests came in the form of land, and so many monasteries became major landowners. They rented out land to tenants to farm, and used the profits to meet their needs. This had two consequences: first, it made well-managed monasteries wealthy institutions; and second, it meant an end to manual labour by the monks themselves. Offices for dead benefactors led to complex liturgies, which left less time for the tripartite structure of the Benedictine Rule. Instead, monks tended to specialize in intellectual labour, most importantly in the copying and composition of texts. Early medieval monasteries represented beacons of light in a largely illiterate society.

The ruins of the Benedictine Abbey of Whitby in north Yorkshire. The abbey was founded in 657 by the abbess Hild (later St. Hilda) who symbolized the Christian tradition in the north of England. Whitby Abbey had a double monastery of monks and nuns and under Hild it gained a great reputation for sanctity. The abbey was destroyed during a Viking invasion but was refounded by Benedictine monks during the 1220s; most of the present ruins date from this period.

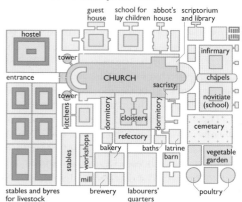

A Benedictine abbey: St.-Gall

guest house • school for lay children • abbot's house • scriptorium and library

hostel

tower

infirmary

entrance

CHURCH

sacristy

chapels

tower

kitchens

dormitory

cloisters

dormitory

novitiate (school)

refectory

cemetary

stables

workshops

bakery

baths

latrine

barn

vegetable garden

mill

stables and byres for livestock

brewery

labourers' quarters

poultry

Benedictine Monasticism

- Catholic territory c. 1150
- Orthodox territory c. 1150
- Muslim territory c. 1150
- pagan territory c. 1150
- major Early Christian Benedictine foundations
- major Carolingian Benedictine foundations (9th century)
- other important Benedictine foundations
- Benedictine foundations with significant royal patronage
- major Benedictine nunneries
- chief Cluniac house
- major Cluniac houses

Entanglement with lay society also had an effect on the governance of monasteries, which became increasingly aristocratic institutions. It was common in Carolingian Europe for laypeople to be given abbacies, and even when this practice died out in the 10th–12th centuries, many of the great monasteries were run by sons of some the most powerful families in Europe. The most influential Benedictine monastery was Cluny, founded in 910 in southern Burgundy by William, duke of Aquitaine. Cluny was noteworthy from the start for its its dependence on the Pope alone. Cluny had become the head of a network of over 300 dependent houses by the 12th century. The extent of Cluny's involvement in world politics and grandeur of liturgy, however, led to a new reforming movement, beginning in the late-11th century, that sought a return to poverty.

The New Monastic Orders

The first challenge to Benedictine dominance in 11th-century Europe came from Italy, where a group of reforming houses such as Camaldoli, Fonte Avellano and Vallombrosa sought to promote a mixture of reclusive and cenobitic ideals.

> *"All our monasteries should use the same chants, and the same books for divine office ... so that there shall be no discord in our daily actions."*
>
> Charter of Charity

Some of these, notably Romuald's foundation at Camaldoli, which in turn inspired Peter Damiani's hermitage at Fonte Avellano, were influenced by the Greek Orthodox monastic tradition of southern Italy. This wave of reform was linked to the papal reform of the same period; Damiani, for example, became a cardinal. It was in France, however, that reforming ideals entered mainstream monasticism most profoundly. In the 1080s Bruno, a canon of Rheims, founded a hermitage at Chartreuse based on the principle of strict seclusion both from one another and from external society. In 1098, Robert, abbot of Molesme in Burgundy, left his abbey after failing to persuade his monks to return to a literal observance of Benedictine Rule. The schismatic monks set up the 'New Monastery' at Cîteaux and Cistercian reforms spread rapidly throughout Europe.

Cistercian Reform

The keynote of Cistercian reform was a return to manual labour, required in the Benedictine Rule but long since forgotten. Linked to this was the refusal to accept or settle on land that was already occupied and under cultivation, and which entailed an income from rents or tithes. As they could not use tenant labour, the Cistercians used lay-brothers, or *conversi,* to farm their lands. The Cistercians took pride in returning to the principle of poverty, in contrast to the wealth they saw in monasteries like Cluny. To emphasize their purity, they adopted white habits, and built churches with minimal decoration. Monastic writing of the 12th century was marked by rhetorical debates about the virtues of reform as opposed to tradition, which historians have traditionally seen as representing the positions of Cistercians and Cluniacs. At the heart of this debate lay the question of how Benedictine Rule should be observed: either according to a literal reading, or allowing for the accumulated traditions that had arisen over time.

Central Organization

The Cistercians were the most successful of the new orders in organizational terms. Their early constitutional documents, such as the Charter of Love (*c.* 1119) and the Statutes (1134), emphasize the centralizing tendency of the new Order. A strict hierarchy prevailed over which the abbot of Cîteaux presided, followed by the abbots of the first four daughter-houses, each of which oversaw its own daughter-houses. All abbots were required to attend the annual chapter-generals and to enforce the agreed statutes. Recent studies have suggested that this organization owes more to ideals than to reality, and shed doubt on the early dating of these documents. Many Cistercian houses, such as Furness in Cumbria, joined the Order through incorporation rather than foundation as daughter-houses. The first half of the 12th century saw a multitude of such reform

A Carthusian Priory: Mount Grace

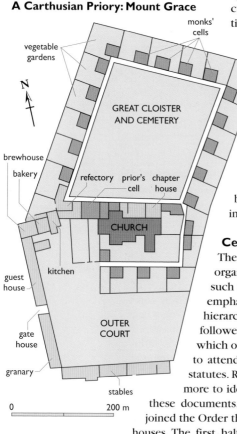

- vegetable gardens
- monks' cells
- GREAT CLOISTER AND CEMETERY
- N
- brewhouse
- bakery
- refectory
- prior's cell
- chapter house
- CHURCH
- kitchen
- guest house
- gate house
- granary
- OUTER COURT
- stables

0   200 m

The New Monastic Orders

🏰 senior Cistercian abbey

🏰 chief Cistercian daughter-houses (founded 1112–20)

🏰 other major Cistercian abbeys

🏰 Premonstratensian houses

🏰 major Carthusian houses

🏰 major Savignac houses

🏰 major Gilbertine houses

🏰 major Camaldolese houses

▦ Catholic territory c. 1150

▦ Orthodox territory c. 1150

▦ Muslim territory c. 1150

▦ pagan territory c. 1150

Rievaulx Abbey, the first Cistercian abbey in North Yorkshire (1131), symbolizes the importance of monasticism in medieval England. Under abbot Aelred (1147–67) it had 140 monks and over 500 lay-brothers.

enterprises, not all of them based on the Rule of Benedict. The Premonstratensians, founded by Norbert of Xanten (1127), followed the Rule of Augustine, and undertook parochial and missionary duties. The Gilbertines, founded by Gilbert of Sempringham, comprised double houses of Benedictine nuns alongside Augustinian canons.

Pilgrimage Routes

The cult of saints played an integral role in medieval piety. Saints were people who, following an especially pious life and/or a martyr's death, had assumed a favoured place in heaven, providing an important link between the human and the divine. Pilgrimage to the shrines of saints became increasingly popular from around 1000 and provided the stimulus for important developments in medieval architecture, industry, transport and trade.

The empty tomb of Jesus Christ and the graves of the early Christian martyrs were central to popular devotion from the beginnings of Christianity. As Christianity spread, the tombs of these saints were rarely left intact; their relics, or corporeal remains, along with their fame, gradually dispersed across Europe. Over time, the canon of saints grew steadily, with relics and shrines visible in churches throughout Christendom. Saints were regarded as important intercessors, and devotion to them was thought to result in favourable circumstances, or even miracles, for the supplicant.

Importance of Pilgrimage

Physical proximity to a relic, it was believed, was especially powerful, particularly when a pilgrimage, with all its attendant hardships, was undertaken as well. Vows to visit a shrine were popular as insurance against calamity, acts of penance or in gratitude for answered prayers. Saints could display their darker sides as well, and there are many recorded stories of saintly wrath vented when pilgrimage vows were broken. The most popular medieval pilgrimage destinations were the Holy Land, Rome and Santiago de Compostela in Spain, with access to each made difficult at varying times due to war, political upheaval or religious intolerance. A host of lesser pilgrimage sites existed, among them the shrines of Thomas Becket in Canterbury and the Three Kings at Cologne.

Pilgrimage was not undertaken lightly as it often meant abandoning loved ones and security for a journey fraught with danger and uncertainty. Pilgrims donned traditional garb including a walking staff and hat and received a special blessing on departure. They travelled alone or in groups and generally followed a specified route, stopping at smaller shrines along the way and staying in the numerous hostels which sprang up along the route. Once pilgrims reached their final destinations, they received a badge indicating their status as pilgrims. Although many pilgrims travelled with little money, begging as they went, wealthier people could journey more comfortably. The economic advantage of a location along the route to a major shrine was

View of the Puerta de las Platerias at the Cathedral of St. James at Santiago de Compostela in Spain. Santiago de Compostela was the final destination on the famous medieval way of pilgrimage, the Camino de Santiago (or Way of St. James). It is named after the Apostle James who made converts to Christianity in northwestern Spain and was buried there after his martyrdom. During the 12th and 13th centuries it was designated a Holy Town, as with Jerusalem and Rome, by the Pope.

Pilgrimage Routes to Santiago de Compostela

— major land routes
— sea routes from Britain
● main pilgrimage towns

apparent to tradesmen and religious establishments alike. Aside from food and lodging, money was to be made as a guide or as a guard (burglary was rife), as well as by those involved in the thriving souvenir industry. Pilgrimage also served as an important stimulant in the development of church architecture as churches along the pilgrimage routes were rebuilt to accommodate large numbers of pilgrims. Built or enlarged between *c*. 1000 and *c*. 1150, pilgrimage churches along the route to the shrine of St. James in Compostela incorporate certain features which allow them to be seen as a distinct sub-group of Romanesque architecture. Large, complex east ends, with numerous radiating chapels, extra side aisles throughout and the addition of a fully vaulted gallery passage are frequently found. Each of these features would have eased the circulation of large numbers of people as well as increased the areas within the church where relics or other devotional objects could be displayed. Indeed, pilgrimage had a far greater social, economic and visual impact along the routes to Compostela than to any other major shrine; this primarily reflects the extreme difficulty the pilgrim faced in reaching Rome or Jerusalem for much of the medieval period.

Romanesque and Gothic Cathedrals

Medieval churches and castles, whether built in the solid, imposing Romanesque style or soaring to incredible Gothic heights, are testaments to the architectural vision and ingenuity of European society during the Middle Ages.

"Once the new rear part is joined to that in front,

The church shines with its middle brightened.

For bright is the part paired brightly with the bright part,

And bright is the noble building which is pervaded by new light ... "

Abbot Suger's inscription for the new choir of the Church of Saint-Denis (1144) from *The Book of Suger*

A view of the nave interior of Vézelay Abbey in Burgundy, France. This 12th-century church is a masterpiece of Romanesque architecture.

Romanesque and Gothic, like so many descriptive historical terms, postdate the styles themselves and were initially intended in a derogatory sense. 'Romanesque' describes the arts and architecture of the period following the final breakdown of the Carolingian empire, and first occurs early in the 19th century in a discussion of Norman architecture and its misinterpretation of classic Roman style. 'Gothic' was applied to the style which prevailed in the High and Later Middle Ages (1150–1500) already during the Renaissance, when stained glass, complex surface decoration and function largely obscured by form and embellishment were seen as irrational and even barbaric.

Romanesque Use of Stone

Romanesque buildings are often disparaged relative to their Gothic descendants, but in their own day they must have been awe-inspiring. They represented new, or at least rediscovered, building technology which championed the use of stone, more long-lasting and imposing than wood and stucco. Romanesque church interiors, with their thick walls, stout load-bearing piers and barrel-vaulted ceilings spanned larger, higher spaces than earlier medieval buildings. Liturgical developments of the period, due to the growing number of priests and the popularity of pilgrimage, added to the grandeur of the Romanesque style by stimulating the need for a proliferation of altars and interior chapels which resulted in ever more complex east ends for cathedrals and churches. Increasingly, smaller parish churches were also built in a similar style.

Gothic architecture is seen as beginning in the Ile-de-France in the second quarter of the 12th century. Its popularity was ensured when the east end of the Abbey of Saint-Denis, chosen by the Capetians as their dynastic mausoleum, was rebuilt by Abbot Suger. The great heights of Gothic cathedrals, with their vast expanses of stained glass and minimal walls changed the face of medieval architecture. Inside a Gothic cathedral one finds a dramatic, glittering jewellery box, an earthly approximation of heaven; outside, the vast, soaring skeletal structure, seemingly supported only by delicately wrought buttresses, announces a building which could apparently be erected only with the help of angels.

Variations of Gothic Style

The Gothic style spread quickly through the rest of Europe, with the basic Gothic tenets of verticality, minimal mural structure to allow for maximum glazing, complicated ribbed vaulting and ornate, although logical, surface decoration remaining despite many regional variations. Early Gothic cathedrals appear fairly logical in their construction, with piers, columns and colonettes seeming to perform a given load-bearing task. Later Gothic buildings mask this initial trend with increasingly complex surface decoration. The Parisian Gothic variant known as Rayonnant, popular from *c.* 1240 through the 14th century, emphasizes light and decoration at the expense of restrained separation of storeys, while late Gothic monuments in the French Flamboyant style cast aside the structural logic of earlier Gothic forms in favour of extreme surface decoration. In England, variations include the Decorated style, inspired by French Rayonnant buildings but with a new proliferation of surface ornament, and the Perpendicular style, in which structural supports, including vaulting, are encased within flattened grids of rectilinear tracery. The Gothic hall church, in which the aisles and the nave are vaulted at the same height to create a unified, open interior, found great favour in Germany. The Gothic style was never popular in Italy, where the ancient preference for classical, Roman rounded arches and mural expanses endured throughout the medieval period.

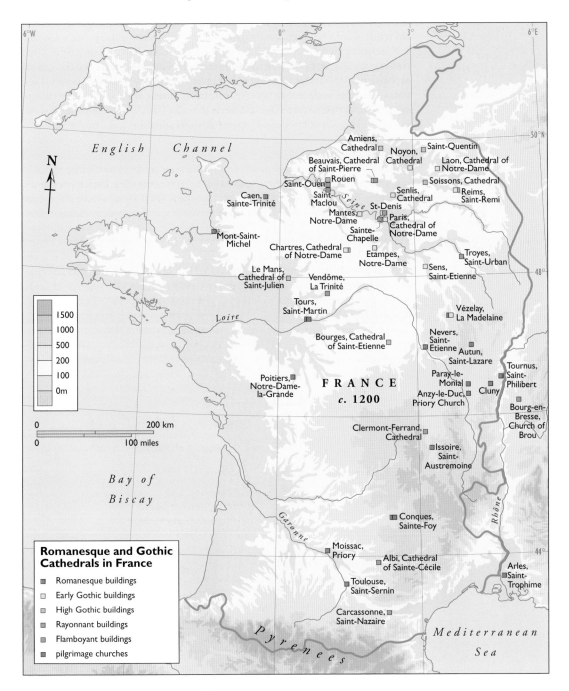

Romanesque and Gothic Cathedrals in France

- Romanesque buildings
- Early Gothic buildings
- High Gothic buildings
- Rayonnant buildings
- Flamboyant buildings
- pilgrimage churches

Castles

> *"My heart fills with joy when I see strong castles under siege ... and knights drawing up on the banks between the lines of palisades.*"
>
> Bertrand de Born,
> 'I Love the Happy
> Eastertide'

Castles developed out of late Roman and early medieval fortified structures. From around 1000 until the end of the 13th century they played a crucial role in the defence and protection of landholdings from small manors to entire kingdoms.

The first castles in Europe were built in France, east of the Loire river, in the 10th century. They were made of wood and often consisted of a mound (or 'motte'), on which could be built one or more towers, circled by a deep ditch and culminating in a high earthen bank (or 'bailey'). Motte and bailey castles were often sited on the highest points in the landscape to allow soldiers to see the enemy at a distance. The area within the bailey grew over time to provide space for soldiers, residents and local people. This protection was often crucial in a Europe where feudal rights were disputed by rival families, landless knights roamed the country in search of booty, and powerful rulers sought to enlarge their lands.

New Technology

The major developments in castle and fortification architecture in Europe during this period resulted from technological advances developed during the Crusades. The first important change was the switch from wooden to stone structures. The successful First Crusade led to a spate of castle building within

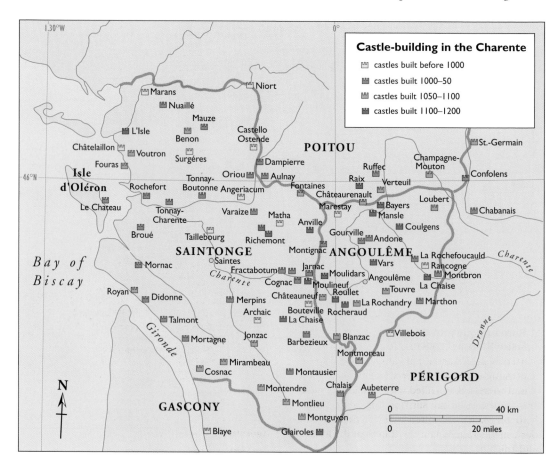

Caerphilly Castle in Wales is one of the great medieval castles of western Europe. It was the first truly concentric castle in Britain when it was built in the late-13th century and made large-scale use of water as defence. Strongly-fortified castles were largely abandoned by 1300 in the face of mounting construction costs and the ever-improving range of artillery available to attacking forces.

the newly-founded Crusader states and, largely because of the shortage of timber in the vicinity, stone became the primary building material. It was recognized almost immediately as a preferable material to wood as it was extremely durable and could not be damaged by fire. Stone castles quickly appeared in Europe, but their inhabitants did not experience the advantage for long, as advances in weaponry also arrived from the East, including the siege tower, a huge structure which could be wheeled alongside a castle to make entry or bombardment easier, and 'Greek fire', an incendiary mixture which spontaneously combusted and could not be extinguished by water.

Defending Castles

Mining the new stone walls and towers led to the addition of much deeper moats to protect the central structures, and traditional square towers (or 'donjons') were soon abandoned for round ones which were harder to scale and provided panoramic views. The wooden drawbridge, which could be raised against invaders, and the portcullis, a metal grille which could be lowered to seal off the inner precinct, could be found in most castles, as could crenellations, which protected archers and crossbowmen, and machicolations, which allowed soldiers to drop things on the enemy below. Concentric castles with a central compound ringed by a series of ditches and walls were also used and, during the 13th century, castles began to be sited at the edge of a high peak with a sheer drop to the back and all the defence structures, like a gatehouse, at the front. Such complex castles were a far cry from the cruder structures of the 10th and early 11th centuries.

The inhabitants of a medieval castle included the knights and soldiers from the household army, servants and the resident family. Surrounded by high walls and guard towers, the residential complex included kitchens, storage areas, living quarters, a chapel and the great hall, a large space for feasting and other entertainments. The open central courtyard was filled with animals, servants and visitors, while the surrounding fields within the outer walls were often used for training and tournaments to maintain the fitness of the household knights.

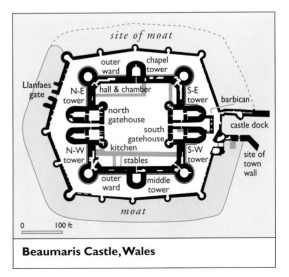

Beaumaris Castle, Wales

Universities and Intellectual Life

The years around 1200 saw the formal beginning of the university system of higher education. With the implementation of set curricula, standardized texts and recognized degrees of achievement, the early universities set in place a format which survives, largely unchanged, in all modern universities.

Education for much of the Middle Ages was a rather casual affair; most people received no formal education, instead learning their trades through apprenticeships or from family members. Each diocese was supposed to run a school, but despite evidence of the existence of some very impressive cathedral schools, there is no proof that all bishops were able to offer this service. Most monasteries appear to have operated schools, although these were largely attended by those preparing to take monastic vows and their teaching focused primarily on theology and liturgy. The very wealthy could hire private tutors, and for the academically-inclined pupil with family support, there were masters who moved from city to city, giving lectures and taking on students at a more advanced level.

The First Universities

Such independent teachers were generally required to obtain a teaching licence from the local bishop. There was as yet no syllabus of study and no degrees were conferred. Partly in an attempt to wrest control of higher education from the Church, and in so doing to promote more open debate, groups of peripatetic masters and their students from the last quarter of the 12th century onwards joined together to establish independent schools in major cities. Initially they received strong support from secular rulers, and increasingly from the Church itself. As students attained certain levels, they were formally examined and awarded titles, such as Master or Doctor, which gradually took the place of the earlier teaching licences and allowed them to teach throughout Europe. The universities at Paris, specializing in theology, and Bologna, specializing in law, were incorporated before 1200. These were quickly followed by others, nearly all set up to train clerics, so teaching theology, but specializing in areas such as medicine, law, the sciences and philosophy. The general course of study was based on the writings of ancient philosophers and early Christian theologians.

Adapted from that already in place in most cathedral schools, it included Latin, liturgy, scriptural exegesis, and the liberal arts, consisting of the *trivium* (grammar, rhetoric and logic) and the *quadrivium* (arithmetic, geometry, harmonics and astronomy).

Student life at a medieval university did not differ greatly from its modern equivalent. Courses were taught through a series of lectures on set texts followed by disputations in which students and masters applied strict rules of logic to ascertain the truth of

This miniature shows Henry of Germany delivering a lecture at the University of Bologna, one of the oldest universities in Europe. Some images of educational life are timeless: in this 14th-century classroom some students are paying attention while others are chatting to each other or even asleep.

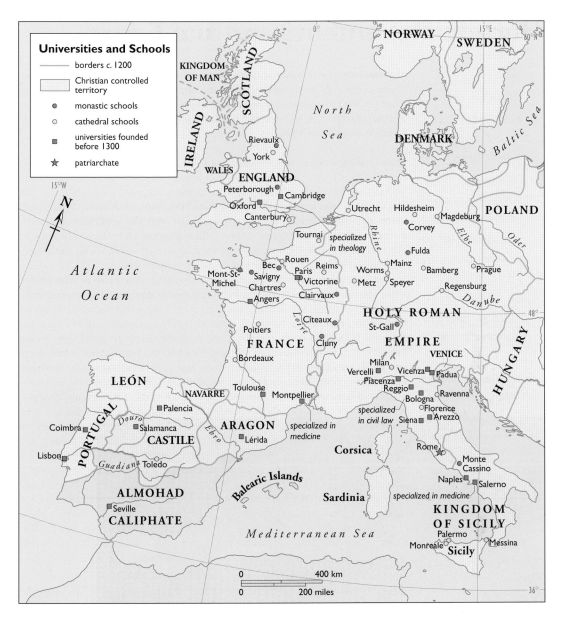

Universities and Schools

— borders c. 1200

▢ Christian controlled territory

● monastic schools

○ cathedral schools

▪ universities founded before 1300

★ patriarchate

given texts. The philosophical method of questioning, primarily developed by Thomas Aquinas at Paris in the 13th century, was the starting point for debate. Known as scholasticism, it allowed questioning to gain understanding of Christian dogma, while recognizing that faith transcends rational thought. Upon completion of a course of study, students were examined by public oral questioning before gaining their degrees. The need for more copies of set texts led to a growth of the lay book trade in the 13th century. Certified copies of texts were made available by university authorities to ensure accuracy, and from the late-12th century the biblical canon was codified and the division of biblical books into chapters became the norm. Finances caused students the same concerns they do today, and in surviving letters to their sons at university medieval parents listed familiar complaints against inappropriate behaviour, excessive drinking and lack of studious application.

Heretic Movements and the Friars

From about the middle of the 12th century, the spread of unorthodox beliefs in many parts of Europe was causing apprehension in the Church. The main reason for the growth of heresy was probably dissatisfaction on the part of the laity with the performance of the Church at parish level.

"The heretics show off their piety, living the Gospel in poverty and austerity, and thus they persuade the ignorant to follow them. ... [You should] ... put false piety to flight by living a truly holy life."

Jordan of Saxony, *The Origins of the Order of Preachers*

Many priests were poorly educated and ill-equipped morally for their office. Heresy fed off anti-clericalism, and was linked to demands for moral reform within the Church. Two major heretical movements were particularly influential: the Waldenses and the Cathars. The Waldenses, or 'Poor of Lyon', were followers of Peter Valdes, a merchant who gave away his wealth and embarked on a life of preaching reform. Denied a licence to preach by the archbishop of Lyon, he and his followers were increasingly drawn from criticizing the Church as an institution to denying the validity of the sacraments.

The Cathars, in contrast, proposed an alternative theology to Catholicism based on the dualist principle that the universe is governed by two powers – evil, which controls all created matter, and good, controlling the spiritual world. Cathars sought to live as simply as possible: their priests, the 'perfect', were vegans who abstained from sex and lived austerely. Both groups found strong followings in the urban areas of northern Italy and southern France, where there was little centralized political authority. By the 1190s much of southern France was openly Cathar in sympathy, and the Cathars had an ecclesiastical network to rival that of the Church.

The Confirmation of the Rule of the Order of St. Francis by Pope Honorius III in 1223. The fresco's painter, Ghirlandaio (1449–94), was one of the great masters of the Florentine school.

The most effective strategy used by the Church to combat heresy was to improve preaching and the provision of the sacraments in the parishes. The leader in this reform was Dominic Guzman, a Spanish Augustinian canon who founded a community of preachers in Toulouse before 1209. The Order of Preachers

(Dominicans) soon spread across areas where heresy had taken root. The aim of the Order was twofold: to ensure that the Christian message was preached effectively, and to train future preachers to supplement the work of the parish priesthood. Consequently, the Order placed special value on theological learning, and by the mid-13th century had begun to dominate the universities of Paris and Oxford. Dominican friars lived in urban priories, following the Augustinian Rule which allowed them to combine communal life with study and preaching.

St. Francis of Assisi

Francis of Assisi, a contemporary of Dominic Guzman, followed a similar path to that of Peter Valdes, forgoing a mercantile career for a life of poverty and preaching. To a greater degree than Dominic, Francis emphasized poverty as an end in itself, and his aim was to provide an example of the Christian life through imitating the Apostles. Although Francis promoted the Christian message as a means of combatting heresy, his mission sought a broader reform of society. Francis' complete rejection of wealth, his lively preaching and powerful personality made a profound impression on those who came into contact with him. Francis combined his uncompromising apostolic life with absolute theological orthodoxy. Unlike Dominic, he was a layman, and he envisaged his order as a lay fellowship working with the priesthood. But, by the mid-13th century the Franciscan Order was becoming more clerical, and, like the Dominicans, had begun to dominate urban Christianity in the later Middle Ages. The Franciscans adopted a conventual life, but for much of the later Middle Ages the Order was troubled about how fully Francis' strictures on poverty should be followed.

Heretic Movements and the Friars

borders c.1200

Orthodox areas

Latin Christendom

area of Bogomils

area of Cathars (Albigensians)

● major Bogomil centres

○ major Cathar (Albigensian) centres

● Waldensian centres

■ first major Franciscan foundation

■ first major Dominican foundation

European Jewry

The dispersal of Jews from the Roman province of Palestine following the uprisings of the 2nd century led to the establishment of Jewish settlements across the Mediterranean world. On the whole, the Romans left the Jews to follow their own customs in peace, as long as those customs were not seen as a threat to imperial rule.

"Philip [Augustus] began to burn with zeal against the Jews ... he ordered that all the Jews in his kingdom should be arrested in their synagogues, and that their gold, silver and fine clothing should be stripped from them, just as the Jews had plundered the Egyptians during their exodus from Egypt."

Rigord, *Life of Philip Augustus*

Early medieval Germanic kings largely followed this practice, treating the Jews as one of the disparate communities under their protection. The sole exception was Visigothic Spain (589–711), where persecution of Jews was endemic. After the Arab conquest of Spain, however, the Jewish communities of Moorish cities like Toledo were revived. Sephardic Jewish culture thrived under the intellectual stimulus provided by the caliphate of Córdoba, while Jews became prominent in medicine, philosophy and natural science as well as in mercantile crafts.

Persecution Begins

In most of western Europe, however, where Christian culture was dominant, Jewish culture was restricted to religious scholarship. An important new school of rabbinical theology developed in France under Rashi (1040–1105), and from the mid-12th century the Hassidic tradition of ascetic piety grew in Germany. Jewish theologians were influential in stimulating Christian theology in the revival of learning in 12th-century cathedral schools, but paradoxically, it was also during this period that anti-Jewish persecutions began. The stimulus for persecution was the preaching of the Crusades. In 1096, the German Count Emich of Leinigen initiated a massacre of Jews in Rhineland towns by crusaders en route for the East; similar massacres were provoked by the preaching of the Second Crusade (1147) in the same area, and in England, recruitment for the Third Crusade in 1189–90 sparked persecutions in London and York. Such outbreaks were in part motivated by resentment at perceived Jewish prosperity. Both the English and French royals encouraged Jews to engage in money-lending, knowing that church law forbade Christians from the trade and also that they could benefit by levying arbitrary taxes on the Jewish communities under their protection. This happened particularly in England, where the Jews were largely restricted to money-lending, and became impoverished by crown taxation. In 1182 Philip II of France expelled Jews from royal lands, but allowed them to buy back their right of abode; in England, the crown gave protection to Jews until 1290, when they were expelled. In Germany, the lack of centralized authority meant that Jews could not be as easily expelled, but they suffered increasing persecutions during the 13th and 14th centuries.

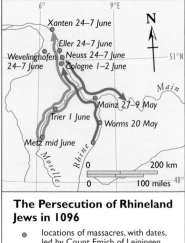

The Persecution of Rhineland Jews in 1096

- locations of massacres, with dates, led by Count Emich of Leiningen
- movements of Count Emich's army
- movements of the breakaway group

(map labels:) Xanten 24–7 June; Eller 24–7 June; Wevelinghofen 24–7 June; Neuss 24–7 June; Cologne 1–2 June; Mainz 27–9 May; Trier 1 June; Worms 20 May; Metz mid June

A detail from Paulo Uccello's painting 'The Miracle of the Desecrated Host' (1465–69) shows the burning of the Jew's house and his family.

The Church's official attitude to the Jews, which derived from the theology of Augustine of Hippo (354–430), was ambiguous. Although the special role of the Jews in sacred history was acknowledged, Jews were also blamed for the death of Christ. The 13th-century papacy introduced restrictions on the clothing, movement and professional activity of Jews, and launched denunciations against the Torah and Talmud. This attitude influenced popular perceptions, and the 'blood libel', the conviction that an international conspiracy of Jews was organizing the murder of Christian children, resulted in hysterical outbreaks of anti-Jewish sentiment. These tended to peak at times of crisis such as the Black Death, for which in the popular imagination Jews were blamed.

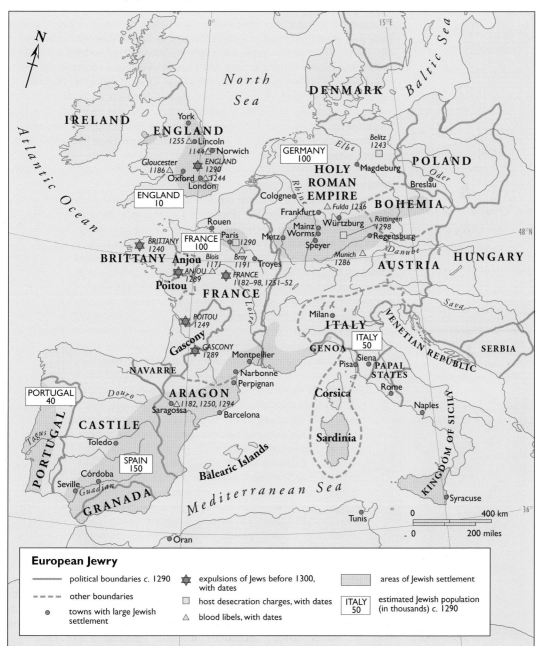

European Jewry

——— political boundaries c. 1290	✡ expulsions of Jews before 1300, with dates
- - - - other boundaries	▢ host desecration charges, with dates
● towns with large Jewish settlement	△ blood libels, with dates
▨ areas of Jewish settlement	
ITALY 50 estimated Jewish population (in thousands) c. 1290	

The Medieval Economy

During the early medieval period economic power was concentrated in the countryside and dominated by the large landowners, but from the 11th century onwards an economy based increasingly on money emerged. By the 15th century, commerce and industry were fast expanding, shifting economic capability to the towns and cities.

"[Pope Lucius III] granted the people of Lucca the right to mint coinage. In ... Tuscany, the Campagna, Romagna, and Apulia. ... This money became more common ... and he ordered everyone living there ... to use that money in their business."

Ptolemy of Lucca

This 14th-century illustration shows the distribution of grain in Florence. There were recurring bouts of famine in the early 14th century in Europe due to the limitations of long-distance transport and trade.

The medieval workforce in many ways remained quite static with the vast majority of the population working the land despite urbanization of the economy. Rural social structures reveal little real change; serfs tied to the land they farmed for their feudal lord gained a few more rights and emerged at the end of the Middle Ages closer to tenant farmers, but both they and the landowners kept to the established status quo. The cities began similarly, with financial power based on land ownership, but quickly a new class of entrepreneurs, whose extensive wealth was in goods, services and hard currency, demanded a respectable position within the urban social structure. The merchant class took control of the European economy, stimulating long-distance trade, consumerism and financial speculation, and it is to them that the financial structures of our modern economy are owed.

Mercantilism

Merchants had existed earlier in the Middle Ages as isolated salesmen travelling from one local market to the next with varied goods, such as cloth, furs or spices, which could not be produced locally. As more permanent markets grew up in the larger towns and cities, merchants established bases and began to act as selling agents for individual commodities. Merchants in each city soon formed guilds which oversaw trade practices within individual cities and which required membership of anyone who wished to sell or trade goods there. By the 13th century guilds often controlled local governing councils.

Craft guilds, which controlled the prices and quality of items produced by various artisans, appeared soon after the merchant guilds. Craft guilds established monopolies and instituted strict systems of training to ensure that their products reached an accepted standard. A prescribed period of apprenticeship, itself often open only to relatives of existing guild members, was followed by time as a journeyman working for wages in a recognized workshop. Upon the production of an item considered to be of high enough quality, a journeyman could become a master and thus earn the right to operate his own workshop. Craft guilds existed for most organized professions including apothecaries, furriers and jewellers, and like the merchant guilds, could wield impressive political power should an overzealous city council threaten their rights.

A rise in demand for luxury goods fostered the growth of international trade. Smaller markets still sold the rural population the produce they required, along with some goods unavailable locally such as woollen cloth, linen or salt, but larger fairs in cities served as centres for the trade of luxury goods such as silks and spices. Merchants dealing in such items needed organized hierarchies of buyers, shipping agents and salesmen as

well as established trade routes, both over land and by sea. Appropriate systems of accounting and payment also became necessary and by the 13th century organized international banking was also underway. The Italians, with their long history of urban settlement and close links via Venice and Sicily to the Byzantine empire, became the earliest leaders in international finance. The first European banks and early advances in bookkeeping can both be traced to Italian merchant families.

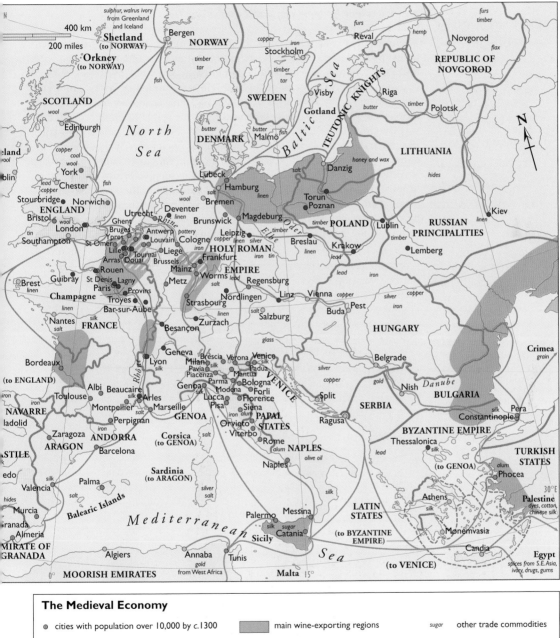

The Medieval Economy

- cities with population over 10,000 by c.1300
- town or city with important trade fair

main wine-exporting regions

main grain-exporting regions

main textile-manufacturing areas

sugar other trade commodities

borders c.1300

major trade routes

The Medieval Countryside

Before World War II, much of the European countryside would have been recognizable to its medieval inhabitants. Despite the land enclosure of later centuries, field divisions and farming patterns remained largely unchanged until the 1940s when the introduction of intensive farming and modern machinery forced the removal of many ancient hedgerows, walls and other field boundaries.

"At Chauvency a lawyer called Alberic demanded labour services that were not due [to the lord], and threatened the serfs of the monastery so that when one poor man's cow miscarried while ploughing, the man himself pulled its yoke all day instead."

Chartes de l'Abbaye de Saint-Hubert en Ardenne (1081)

The open-field system served as the basis of European farming from ancient times through to the early modern period. Large areas of common land were divided into strips which could be bounded by low walls or hedges or, more commonly, simply by low ridges of earth. The patterns left by such divisions are still visible in many rural areas of Britain, Scandinavia and continental Europe. Strips were probably farmed communally, but the resulting produce from each was the property of a specific farmer or family. Strips were generally of equal size, often defined as an 'acre' in contemporary documents; widths were determined by a local standard measure. Legal documents tend to refer to the strips according to their location relative to that of the sun overhead ('near the sun', 'toward the sun', etc.), and this practice is indicated in the Scandinavian law-term *solskifte* or 'sun division'. In some parts of Europe these strips appear to have been passed to a different family each year, thus encouraging all to contribute to the maintenance of the communal field, but elsewhere designated

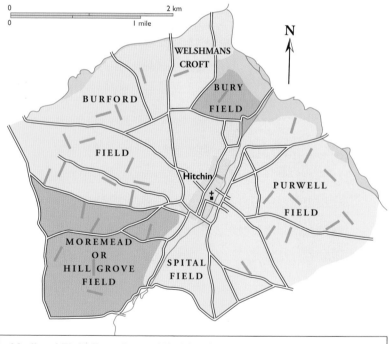

Medieval Field-Rotation at Hitchin, Hertfordshire

- permanent pasture
- grain – first year of rotation
- grain – second year of rotation
- fallow – third year of rotation
- dwelling, outbuilding or vegetable gardens
- Individual dwelling with outbuildings, yards, vegetable gardens and allocated cultivation strips

An aerial view of Laxton in Nottinghamshire. The village is unique in England for continuing to use the open-field system of farming, in which fields are divided between the villagers into strips to ensure that the best land is fairly shared. The three-field system of roatation between crops, fallow and pasture is evident in this late evening view in the different colours of the fields.

parcels were passed down through families. In areas where feudalism was strong, the local lord would receive more than the single strip designated to each tenant or perhaps a share of that grown on each strip within a given field.

In the early Middle Ages, villages operated the two-field system of cultivation. Imported from the Middle East, this form of crop rotation allowed one field to be farmed while the second was grazed by livestock. The fallow field was given a 'rest', and the animal droppings helped to restore nutrients to the soil.

The Three-Field System

By the Carolingian period the new three-field system had begun to spread from the area between the Loire and the Rhine rivers to the rest of Europe. The addition of a third field had a number of advantages. First, it allowed more of the available arable land to be cultivated, leaving only one third, rather than one half, of the land fallow each year. The two cultivated fields could be planted with crops harvested in the autumn (barley, oats or legumes) and in the spring (barley, wheat or rye), allowing two separate harvests and alleviating the danger of complete crop failure inherent in a single harvest. Grazing areas could be changed after each harvest and extra oats and grain could be used as silage for livestock. Farming technology also improved greatly from this period, with major developments in the plough and the switch from oxen to horses to provide pulling power.

Open arable land in the European countryside was increasingly used for agricultural purposes, but many areas unsuitable for farming remained largely untouched. Medieval literature and art show the countryside was used for recreational pastimes, particularly by the gentry and nobility who appear riding, hunting and courting in idyllic rural settings. A similar rosy picture is painted of peasants whose endless toil and hand-to-mouth existence is often portrayed as one of simple pleasures taken among the fertile fields of the countryside. No doubt the romanticizing of the countryside popular in the ancient world and still prevalent today also informed our medieval ancestors.

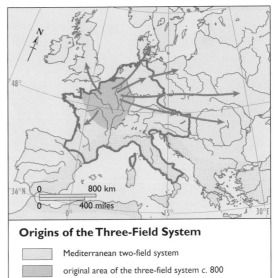

Origins of the Three-Field System

- Mediterranean two-field system
- original area of the three-field system c. 800
- Carolingian empire c. 814
- spread of the three-field system

The Growth of Towns

*"The new consuls
... must select
one good man,
who will then
select two even
better men ... who
are more suitable;
these will then
swear to elect six
councillors for
the commune,
and a treasurer, a
notary, overseers,
a treasurer for
the customs house
and dispatchers. "*

Statutes of Volterra
(1224)

Cities all over Europe experienced rapid physical and economic growth in the 11th and 12th centuries. Many new cities were founded, primarily as ports and trading centres, but the consolidation and expansion of the older, more established urban settlements had the greatest impact on the development of the modern map of Europe.

Nearly all cities in medieval Europe occupied the sites of earlier settlement. Many were laid over Roman foundations, others sat on top of more ancient ruins, while still others, primarily in regions outside of Roman imperial boundaries, developed out of small settlements of indigenous peoples. Some of these earlier towns and cities had enjoyed continuous occupation from their inception. Cities on the Italian peninsula are often good examples of this, and their Roman features (walls, streets and buildings) generally served as the basis for a fairly organic growth as the Middle Ages progressed. Many cities had less straightforward histories, with several periods, not always contiguous, of occupation by different peoples, serving perhaps once as a trading centre and later as a border outpost. Regardless of their earlier incarnations, the larger, commercial urban settlements exhibit similar patterns of growth as their populations swelled to meet the demands of increasing trade and commerce in the years after 1000.

Urban Expansion

On the eve of the period of urban growth, the surviving features of any former occupations varied greatly from city to city. A well-preserved Roman city might come complete with extensive surviving walls, a logical street layout and even civic amenities such as bridges and public spaces which could be utilized for markets or new

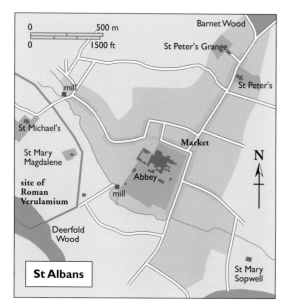

St Albans

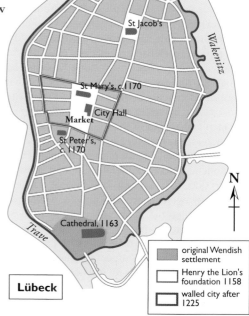

Lübeck

original Wendish settlement

Henry the Lion's foundation 1158

walled city after 1225

buildings. Medieval cities occupying the sites of earlier defensive outposts or fortified residences generally possessed little more than some defensive walls, either rebuilt (probably badly) in the early medieval period or in need of extensive refurbishment. Such cities, which include most of the new trading cities established along the Baltic coast and in central and eastern Europe, at times developed along the layout already dictated by pre-existing structures or institutions; thus a seigneurial residence, church or monastery could determine the location of a new market or commercial area.

Other cities were more impressively 'refounded' as they were modernized into commercial centres. The location of the city centre was sometimes relocated or existing streets and buildings reconfigured to suit the demands of the new concentration of trade and commerce within the city.

The Function of City Walls

Although city walls by the central Middle Ages played defensive roles, they were equally important for regulating access to the city centre. Walls were expensive to build or repair and once erected could not meet the demands of a quickly growing population. Communities of artisans, called faubourgs, developed just outside the walls, and over time these grew into large quarters or suburbs. As these areas were incorporated within the city, subsequent encircling walls might be erected, leading to the growth of new faubourgs.

The Plan of Rome from the sumptuous *Très Riches Heures du Duc de Berry*, painted in the 15th century. The medieval Book of Hours was primarily a collection of the text for each liturgical hour of the day.

Such concentric development is apparent in the layouts of many medieval cities, but early walls did not always define the regions within a city. In some instances quarters within the city centre simply expanded to the area on the other side of the wall which could then be knocked through or demolished; in others certain artisans could relocate entirely to a new area leaving their old quarter to be taken over by others. Regardless of the ways in which they developed, the European city had taken shape by the 13th century; few new cities can be dated to after 1200, and most established cities continued to grow out of the urban plans in place by this date.

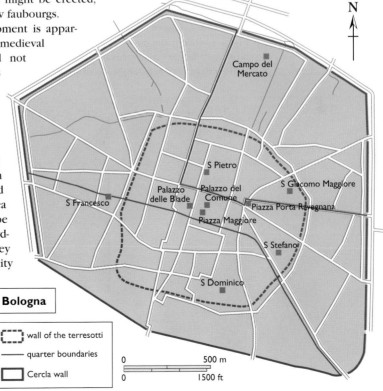

N

Bologna

- [- - -] wall of the terresotti
- —— quarter boundaries
- [ ] Cercla wall

Campo del Mercato

S Pietro

Palazzo delle Blade

Palazzo del Comune

S Giacomo Maggiore

Piazza Porta Ravegnana

S Francesco

Piazza Maggiore

S Stefano

S Dominico

0   500 m
0   1500 ft

Flanders and the Cloth Industry

Although the textile industry in Flanders was of major importance for the economy of medieval Europe, it played a decreasing role in international trade as the Middle Ages progressed.

"I, Jean, countess of Flanders and Hainault ... and my successors will not demand any toll or tax from any fifty wool weavers who come to Courtrai henceforth. And this shall remain the case for their lifetimes."

Charter of the Counts of Flanders (1224)

Cloth, and its weaving and finishing, was much associated with medieval Flanders, although contemporary sources suggest that wool came from outside. The relatively urban area of Flanders lacked the acreage necessary for large-scale sheep breeding and, as the industry grew and Flemish grazing land was turned to arable use, the demand for wool far outstripped the production of local sheep farmers. England, with Scotland and Ireland, provided most of the wool for Flemish weavers, dyers and fullers. Until the 13th century, a balanced trade relationship between England and Flanders allowed both economies to flourish, with England exporting wool and importing, via Flemish merchants, textiles, spices and other goods. The European market for Flemish cloth was crucial for Flanders as merchants from France and Italy supplied many of their dyes.

The Three Cities

Although by the 13th century the main centres of cloth production were in the cities of Ghent, Bruges and Ypres, most small towns in Flanders boasted a fair output of fabrics. Ghent, Bruges and Ypres, known as the Three Cities, produced both luxury and less expensive cloth, while most smaller centres specialized in the lower end of the market. As international trade became more formalized, the Three Cities began to concentrate on luxury woollens. The fairs of Champagne served as the first means of selling Flemish goods, with northern European trading centres such as Cologne and Bruges gaining importance over time. After 1277, direct overseas trade with Genoa and other Italian cities meant that the traditional northern fairs became smaller centres of local trade. The replacement of the northern trading fairs by overseas routes run largely by Italians affected most mercantile economies of the era, but of more importance for the Flemish industry was the regularization of trade with England in the later 13th century.

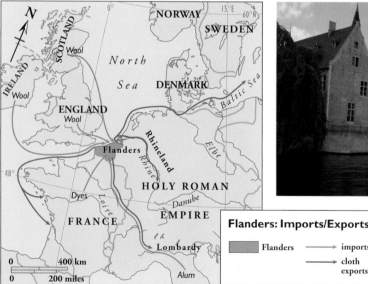

The Quai du Rosaire and the belfry of City Hall in Bruges, Belgium. Bruges was a major cloth-producing centre and the 13th-century belfry was built when the well-preserved medieval city was at its richest.

Flanders: Imports/Exports

Flanders

→ imports

→ cloth exports

Flanders and the Cloth Industry

•••••• border of Flanders *c.* 1150	● centres of castellanies	■ Hanseatic depots
▨ fiefs and protectorates of Flanders	□ main centres of cloth production	✚ bishoprics
── border between France and the Holy Roman empire	□ smaller centres of cloth production	● peer of Flanders
── borders of castellanies	▲ cities with major trade fairs	■ court official of Flanders

The English King Henry III began to demand, on penalty of fines and tariffs, that all Flemish cloth be sold as bolts of equal length and width, and at fair prices. These regulations proved disastrous to the Flemish merchant, largely due to inconsistencies within the Flemish system of production. The dimensions of a piece of fabric, by Flemish convention, often indicated its place of origin, thus making the English regulations very onerous. Quality control also proved difficult as the smaller Flemish towns tried to pass off inferior fabric as the more expensive types made in the Three Cities. The Wool Staple of 1294, which meant that English wool could only leave English territory through designated ports, further tightened English control of the trading relationship. During the 1270s hostilities between England and Flanders escalated; bolts of cloth were seized at English markets and Flemish buyers began getting wool from elsewhere and smuggling much of what had once been legally imported from England. Once these disputes were settled, Flanders had lost most of its earlier trade advantages and mass production of textiles had spread into the surrounding territories.

German Settlement in Eastern Europe

"Although these pagans are evil, their land is excellent .... So, renowned Saxons, Franks, men of Lorraine and Flemings, here is a chance to ... seize the best land in which to live."

Magdeburg Appeal, mid-12th century

With German emperors more interested in extending control over Italy and earning the respect of the great rulers of western Europe, the German princes of the 12th and 13th centuries sought to extend their feudal territories and increase their wealth through eastward expansion. By 1250, the influence of Germanic culture and traditions had spread from the German heartlands to northern territories east of the River Elbe and into Austria, Bohemia and Hungary.

In the 12th century, the *Drang nach Osten*, or 'drive to the east', was spearheaded by Henry the Lion, duke of Bavaria, Saxony and Lüneburg. A member of the Welf dynasty of Bavaria, Henry the Lion agreed in 1154 to support the imperial claims of Frederick I Barbarossa, his cousin and a member of the rival Hohenstaufen family. Henry did much to consolidate his family's position until he was stripped of most of his lands after his fall from power in 1180. Within his duchies he founded new cities, such as Munich in 1157, and revitalized older ones in an attempt to rival the great centres of culture, commerce and learning to the west. To protect his eastern borders and to extend his feudal territories, Henry led raids into Slavic territories, brutally depopulating large areas and resettling them with Germans. His success here also opened up the Baltic Sea to German traders and Henry developed new ports and commercial centres, including Lübeck in 1159, to foster economic growth in the region.

Rival German Dynasties

Such success inevitably led to political unrest, both within Henry's lands and among rival German princes. Henry's power waned from the 1170s and other German dynasties began to assert control over Germany's eastern frontiers. The Ascanian dynasty benefited the most from Henry the Lion's downfall. Margraves (provincial governors) of Brandenburg since 1134, they took much of Saxony east of the Elbe from Henry's supporters and founded two new duchies, Saxe-Wittenburg and Saxe-Lauenburg, the latter of which they would control until the end of the 17th century. Other German nobles also took part in eastward expansion, among them the Babenbergs in Austria, raised from margraves to dukes in 1156 by Frederick I Barbarossa, and the Wettin dynasty in Meissen. In the 13th century, German settlers moved further eastwards into Pomerania, Lusatia and Silesia, territories which had been subdued by the Poles with the help of German mercenaries and where German settlers were for the most part welcomed. Similarly German colonization continued along the western and southern borders of Bohemia and the eastern border of Austria.

At times German settlers chose to travel some distance in return for land and privileges. The Teutonic Knights, a German order founded in the Crusader States in the late 12th century, often supported German colonies within territories that they conquered and converted to Christianity. Even when the Teutonic Order was expelled from Transylvania by its Hungarian overlords, German settlers remained behind and integrated into the indigenous society. German settlers were again caught up in conflict between the Teutonic Knights and territorial rulers in Prussia around 1250. The Polish Prince Conrad in 1226 had asked the Teutonic Knights to help him subdue the neighbouring Prussian people who were threatening his territory of Masovia. The Knights conquered Prussia, began to con-

An image of the medieval German knight-hero Tannhäuser, from the early 14th century Codex Manesse. His depiction in the costume of the Teutonic Knights reflects the extent to which the German colonization of Eastern Europe (led by the Knights) had become a national enterprise in German consciousness by this date.

German Settlement in Eastern Europe

- •••••• border of the Holy Roman empire *c.* 962
- – – – border of the Holy Roman empire *c.* 1400
- ▨▨ land of the Teutonic Knights 1390
- ▨ area of German settlement *c.* 962
- ▨ expansion of German settlement by 1250
- ▨ expansion of German settlement by 1300
- ▨ expansion of German settlement by 1400
- ✝ bishoprics founded 1100–1300
- ● new German towns
- 1242 ✕ battle

vert the Prussians to Christianity and settled Germans along Prussia's western borders. Soon afterwards, in defiance of their agreement to serve as vassals to Prince Conrad, the Knights established a power base at Marienburg (present-day Malbork) and from here would go on to control much of the Baltic region.

English Wars in the British Isles

From the mid-12th century the territorial ambitions of the Angevin dynasty expanded to encompass most of the British Isles. Ireland and Wales were partially conquered, but the kingdom of Scotland proved a much more formidable rival.

"Scottish warriors came ... to raise the English siege [of Dunbar castle]. And when the Englishmen saw them, they fell upon them and discomfited the Scots, and the chase continued more than five leagues away.... And there died ... 10,055 by right reckoning."

Entry for 26 & 27 April 1296 from a journal of the first Scottish campaign of Edward I of England

Early in his reign Henry II re-established control over the parts of northern England lost to the Scots during the reign of King Stephen, and, by his death in 1189, he had secured the overlordship of Ireland. Several Irish kings resisted the feudal system imposed upon them, but their power waned in the face of the civil administration of Ireland begun under King John. By 1300 Ireland had been divided into counties and possessed its own exchequer and parliament. Most of Ireland was controlled, at least nominally, by the English crown for the remainder of the Middle Ages, although Irish independence remained problematic.

In 1301 Edward I awarded Edward, his eldest surviving son and heir, the title of Prince of Wales as a symbol of English domination over the Welsh. Control over the independent Welsh principalities was won by extensive military campaigns; those through the north can be tracked by the imposing castles erected by Edward I as a show of English military power. Many Welsh territories along the border with England had been granted by William the Conqueror to Norman overlords in the 11th century as protection against the powerful princes of Gwynedd, Powys and Deheubarth. Llewelyn ap Gruffudd, prince of Gwynedd, had pledged his feudal allegiance as overlord of Wales to the English king Henry III, but his attempts to wrest land from the marcher barons and the other Welsh princes forced Edward I to enter Wales in 1277. Llewelyn was killed at Irfon Bridge in 1282; his brother Dafydd tried to continue the rebellion, but died the next year. Smaller-scale insurrections in the final decades of the century were quickly put down; by the end of the century Wales had been carved up and added to the shire system, but it was not represented in the English parliament.

Conflict with Scotland

The kingdom of Scotland, through its dealings with England and other kingdoms, occupied a stronger diplomatic position than the Irish kingdoms or the Welsh principalities. While England had struggled with civil war, baronial dissension, economic incompetence and foreign military conflict, Scotland in the 12th and 13th centuries had evolved into a consolidated sovereign territory. When Edward I negotiated a marriage between his son Edward and Margaret, the heir to the Scottish throne, he was recognizing Scotland as a political power which might be joined to England through dynastic alliance, but which could not easily be conquered by force. Margaret's death in 1290 left a power vacuum in Scotland which Edward attempted to turn to his advantage by demanding homage from John Balliol, the newly-crowned king. English invasion of Scotland followed Scottish refusal to accept Edward as overlord; Edward's forces temporarily reduced Scotland to an English dependency. Conquest stimulated unity among the Scots, who under William Wallace and Robert Bruce, displayed a military strength and national pride which took the English by surprise. Following Wallace's defeat of the English at Stirling Bridge, Robert Bruce's ascent to the Scottish throne and his later success at the battle of Bannockburn in 1314, England, now ruled by Edward II, fought back hard. Still Scottish forces triumphed, pushing further into northern England and in 1315 even invading Ireland. A truce between Edward II and Robert Bruce in 1323 ended open conflict, and in 1328 Edward III of England recognized Scotland as a sovereign power.

Caerlaverock Castle is one of Scotland's finest castles. It was often under siege during its turbulent history, including in 1300 by Edward I, and possession of the castle passed several times between the Scots and the English.

English Wars in the British Isles

English territory in 1272

Principality of Wales under Llywelyn ap Gruffudd (Treaty of Montgomery 1267)

independent Irish chiefdoms

O'BRIEN   Irish dynasties

Kingdom of Scotland

castles

Edwardian conquest of Wales

castles begun by Edward 1277–8

Welsh castles captured by Edward 1282–3

castles begun by Edward after the 1282–3 campaign

Edward's campaign of 1282–3

Scottish Wars of Independence

Edward's campaign of 1296

Edward's campaign of 1298

castles captured for Robert Bruce 1307–14

area of northern England subject to Scots raids 1314–28

Bruce invasion of Ireland

Edward Bruce's campaign of 1315

Edward Bruce's campaign of 1317

Earldom of Orkney (to NORWAY)

North Sea

Skelbo
Banff
Elgin
Inverness
Nairn
Slioch 1307
Inverurie 1308
Aberdeen
Inverlochy
Dunstaffnage
Brander 1308
Perth
Dundee
Methven 1306
Stirling
Bannockburn 1314
Dumbarton
Kirkintilloch
Falkirk 1298
Edinburgh
Dunbar
Loudon Hill 1307
Wark
Norham
Berwick
Bamburgh
Dunyveg
Cumnock
Selkirk
Dunaverty
Glen Trool 1307
Caerlaverock
Lochmaben
Northburgh
Coleraine
Connor 1315
Castle Douglas
Carlisle
Newcastle upon Tyne
Stanthorpe Park 1327
O'DONNELL
O'NEILL
Carrickfergus
Penrith
Barnard Castle
Tees
Sligo
MAGUIRE
O'HANLON
MACCARTAN
MACMAHON
Egremont
Richmond
Myton on Swale 1319
O'ROURKE O'REILLY
Fochart 1318
Greencastle
Rushen
Lancaster
Boroughbridge 1322,1327
O'CONNOR
O'FARRELL
Kells 1315
Trim
Drogheda
Skipton
York
Pontefract

Atlantic Ocean

Irish Sea

(claimed by England 1290, control effective by 1333)

Galway
Athenry
Athlone
Athenry 1316
O'CONNOR FALY
Dublin
O'BRIEN
Ardskull 1316
Kilkenny
MACMUIRROUGH
Shannon
Limerick
Wexford
Waterford
MACCARTHY

Conwy
Beaumaris
Rhuddlan
Flint
Ewloe
Chester
Caernarfon 1287
Hope
Dolwyddelan
Dinas Bran
Harlech
Denbigh
Shrewsbury
Castell-y-Bere
Montgomery
Kenilworth
Aberystwyth
Builth
Ludlow
Cardigan
Irfon Bridge 1264
Goodrich
Pembroke
Kidwelly
Berkeley
Caerphilly
Severn
Trent
Thames
Winchester

N

Part III: Latin Europe and its Neighbours

Just as medieval Europe between 1000 and 1300 underwent huge expansions in population and urban development, as agricultural techniques and the crafts of government improved, and culture and learning advanced, so also were its physical and political frontiers pushed beyond their former limits. Europeans on the eve of the second millennium had no knowledge of the neighbouring Islamic world, except in Spain, and they regarded the Byzantine civilization of the eastern Mediterranean with wonder and envy.

East of the Elbe and Danube, and around the Baltic, lived pagan peoples as yet barely touched by contact with Europeans. A world beyond that was known to exist, and a trickle of luxury goods from Islamic lands, or even India, found their way to the courts of Europe, but Europe was neither wealthy, peaceful nor curious enough to take advantage of the possibility of regular long-distance trade.

By 1300, the balance had shifted decisively. To the north and east, European frontiers had expanded to drive the last pagans virtually to extermination; to the south, the borders of Christendom had been pushed almost to the north African coast, while European settlers had established new societies in the eastern Mediterranean. Moreover, new peoples unknown before 1000 in the West had come into the political, cultural and diplomatic orbit of Europe: Armenians, Georgians, Ethiopians, Russians, Poles, Hungarians, Mongols – quite apart from the Muslims and pagans against whom regular wars were waged.

European Urge to Conquer

It is no exaggeration to say that the most distinctive feature of European society in this period was a tendency towards conquest and new settlement in territories previously unaffected by western developments. In some cases, as for example in Eastern Europe, the Baltic, and the Celtic world of the far west, European settlers brought with them more advanced and sophisticated social and political forms. In the south and east, however, Latin expansion represented the dominance of a militarized nobility over largely urban and civic societies whose governmental structures and way of life were to a large degree based on patterns established in the ancient world. Typically, western settlers appeared first as one element in a competitive political environment. In the Iberian Peninsula, southern Italy and the Near East, they were able to take advantage of the recent collapse of central authority, and to profit from the lack of a single concerted opposition to their presence.

The causes behind the western urge to conquer and settle new areas are complex. One factor was certainly the increase in population that led to intensive competition for land in regions that had long been settled. This can be seen most graphically in the example of Norman Sicily, settled initially by only a few families, the most ruthless of which, the Hautevilles, included six sons. It is no surprise to find much of the drive for overseas conquest and settlement coming from regions in which primogeniture (inheritance by the eldest son) had emerging as the normative model of passing on land from one generation to the next. This custom encouraged younger sons to seek new lands outside the political sphere in which they had grown up. This explanation, however, has limitations. Even in the 12th century there were still plenty of uncultivated and unclaimed lands within the traditional confines of the West, and far more energy was expended on the less glamorous tasks of clearing forests and draining marshes to bring new lands under cultivation than in military adventures overseas. Other strategies were available to families than exporting younger sons to the south or east – service in other households, marriage alliances, purchase and so on. Moreover, knights who wanted to take the cross, to embark on a campaign against the Muslims in Spain, or even to travel to southern Italy or the Byzantine empire to seek their fortunes as hired warriors in a regional war, required some initial outlay of capital. Much of the evidence available suggests that such enterprises were often family undertakings. One of the features of western expansion overseas, indeed, is the character that such expeditions have as enterprises based on traditional patterns of relationships between groups and families. If a baron decided, for example, to embark on a crusade, he would recruit his army from among those men who were already his vassals. This meant that feudal loyalties already established in the West might be exported to the new lands, where they could form the basis of new political organizations.

The First Crusade

Another factor in western expansion was ideological. This was most marked in the case of the Crusades to the East, which, although also presenting opportunities for material advancement, began primarily as a spiritual exercise. The Reconquista in Spain and the Baltic Crusades both followed the spiritual rationale set with the preaching of the First Crusade in 1095, but both of these series of wars always retained the strong character of territorial campaigns with which they had begun. In contrast to these, the First Crusade was marked by a strong sense on the part of the participants that by recovering the holy places of Jerusalem from the Turks, they were serving God through a penitential activity. Holy wars had been preached before, but the radical element in 1095 was the coupling of the idea of pilgrimage, traditionally a devotion associated with penitence, with war. The success of the appeal can be explained by a combination of the spare capacity in the West for military enterprise with an emotive piety that saw the Holy Sepulchre as a symbol of Christianity under threat from a dangerous enemy. Two factors thus combined to make the Crusade possible: a pre-existing devotion to Jerusalem as the centre of Christendom, through the long-standing practice of pilgrimage; and the emergence of a penitential system in which the secular knighthood were willing to participate. Settlement of new lands appeared to be a low priority for most who took the cross, for very few

The church of San Miguel de Escalada in Spain. Following a period of Moorish sovereignty in the late-9th to early-10th century, the Asturian king Alfonso III conquered the region of León and commissioned this Mozarabic church. The church was built in 913 by refugee monks from Córdoba and some of its interior architectural features, such as the horseshoe arches, are similar to those of the Great Mosque of Córdoba.

remained behind in 1099. Those who did were, with the exception of a few great nobles, of lesser-ranking landholding families in the West. Thus, although the causes behind the initial conquest of lands in the east were different, the Crusader States provided opportunities for social advancement in the same way as other forms of western expansion in the same period.

Interior of the dome over the mihrab at the Great Mosque in Córdoba, Spain. The mihrab, or inner sanctuary, is topped by this richly decorated mosaic dome which dates to 964. Córdoba was the capital of the Spanish Muslim Umayyad dynasty (756–1031) and the Great Mosque, which took over 200 years to complete, is one of the most magnificent Islamic monuments in Spain.

The preaching of a crusade provided a religious justification for annexing territories held by non-Christians. Thus German crusaders successfully petitioned the Pope to have their vows transferred to a campaign against the pagan Wendish people of Prussia in 1147–48, on the grounds that enforcing the spread of Christianity was in itself a penitential act. Similarly, Spanish Christians were assured that their reconquest of Islamic territory merited the same spiritual rewards as the Crusades to the East. In 1170, Henry II of England even tried to claim that his invasion of Ireland should enjoy similar status, because the Irish, although Christian, were barbaric and unreformed. When the Fourth Crusade turned against Constantinople instead of the Turks, justification was found on the grounds that the Byzantines were schismatic, heretical, and that they obstructed crusading by giving practical aid to the Turks. Crusading therefore became a peg on which rulers and popes could hang aspirations of territorial conquest. Not until the 13th century, however, was a legal rationale found for conquest of non-Christian peoples because they were infidels.

Relations with Byzantium

Territorial expansion necessitated relationships with indigenous peoples of neighbouring lands. Attitudes to non-Latin peoples depended partly on political circumstances and partly on cultural conditioning. Small groups of western knights, particularly Normans and English, had taken service with Byzantine armies since the mid-11th century. But whereas at the beginning of the century Byzantium represented the dominant partner in an unequal relationship, by the time of the First Crusade Byzantine cultural superiority no longer overawed westerners to the same extent. Throughout the period 1000–1300, political, diplomatic and religious exchanges between Byzantium and the West were intertwined. Sometimes, as for example during the reign of the pro-western emperor Manuel Komnenos (1142–80), military co-operation was possible, but most westerners despised what they saw as Byzantine over-sophistication, and distrusted their religious customs. It is difficult to know, however, whether cultural distrust caused or was a consequence of political disagreements, such as that which arose between the Byzantine emperor and the first crusaders. The Latin sack of Constantinople in 1204 was the result of a series of political events, but it is unlikely that it would have happened had a degree of mutual distrust not already been present between westerners and Byzantines.

Western attitudes towards Islam altered significantly during the period 1000–1300. Before the First Crusade, the only region where sustained contact between Muslims and Christians was possible was Spain, where most Christians lived under Islamic rule. The prevailing attitude to Islam was governed by ignorance. By 1100, however, as a result of the Crusade, the ongoing Reconquista in Spain and the Norman conquest of Sicily, large Muslim populations came under Latin rule. Where the impetus for conquest was religious, as in the Crusade, initial treatment was harsh: between 1099 and 1110, the crusaders massacred Muslims in many Palestinian cities, enslaved others, and resettled still more. Eventually, however, Latin settlers developed a more pragmatic attitude with the realization that they needed the indigenous peoples to provide a labour force.

Varying Attitudes to Muslims

Attitudes to subject peoples also varied among westerners. As the 12th-century Muslim writer Usamah ibn-munqidh observed, the longer a Frank lived in the East, the less barbarous, and thus the more tolerant of difference, he became. Similarly, French and Spanish crusaders disagreed over the treatment of defeated Muslims after the battle of Las Navas de Tolosa (1212): the French were in favour of mass slaughter, whereas the Spanish, who were more accustomed to Muslims, merely wanted to rule over them. One major difference between the Crusader States on the one hand and Spain, and to a lesser degree, Sicily, on the other, was that Islam became a largely rural religion under Latin rule in the East. Lacking an urban intelligentsia, or coherent and articulate leadership, Muslims in the Crusader States remained largely passive, and were left alone by their western lords as long as they paid their taxes and feudal dues. They were a tolerated, but second-class population in a society in which the lowest-born Frank was considered in law superior to the highest-born native. In contrast, Muslims under Christian rule in Spain and Sicily formed an important element in government and commerce. The Norman and Hohenstaufen rulers of Sicily in the 12th and 13th centuries even formed Muslim regiments in their armies.

A modern statue of a crusader in Jerusalem, Israel. Jerusalem has long been a holy centre for Christians, Jews and Muslims. By the late-11th century reports of Turkish mistreatment of Christian pilgrims were circulating in Europe. The First Crusade, launched in 1095, led to Jerusalem being captured by the Christians in 1099. Jerusalem remained in Christian hands from 1099 to 1187, and again from 1229 to 1244, after which it was never recaptured by the crusaders. Crusaders came from many different kingdoms; some were driven by greed and many others by devotion.

Indigenous Christians

Across the Mediterranean, Latin conquerors and settlers also had to deal with populations of indigenous Christians who came under their rule. Attitudes to and treatment of these peoples varied. In Spain, the Christian 'Mozarabs', who had over the centuries adopted the Arabic language and developed their own religious traditions separately from the rest of Europe, were regarded with some suspicion, especially by the papacy and by French knights who came to fight in the Reconquista. As the Reconquista became, in the 12th century, increasingly influenced by the religious ideology of crusading, so trans-Pyrenean influences in the Spanish Church became more marked. This happened to a lesser degree in Norman Italy, where the kings, who were usually at odds with the papacy, patronized indigenous Greek Orthodox monasteries in Calabria and Sicily. Orthodoxy remained vibrant throughout the period in Greek-speaking regions of Italy under Latin rule. In the crusader east, the situation for indigenous Christians, most of whom were Arabic-speaking, changed markedly from the 12th to the 13th century. Before the 1190s, indigenous Orthodox populations were largely left alone, and although Latin bishops were imposed over them, the parish structures and settlement patterns of Orthodox communities continued as before. Orthodox monasticism underwent a significant revival under Latin rule, and Orthodox clergy were allowed to officiate at the holy places. In the countryside, there is evidence that some indigenous Christian communities shared churches, and rural resources such as irrigation, with Latin settlers. The crusader conquest of Cyprus in 1191 and of the Byzantine empire in 1204, however, brought populations of Greek rather than Arabic speaking Orthodox Christians under Latin rule, and these fared worse. Attempts were made to bring Orthodox customs and doctrines into line with the Catholic Church, sometimes, as in Cyprus in the 1220s, by force. In Cyprus and the conquered Byzantine territories, western barons replaced Greeks as the major landowners. Socially, politically and economically, these conquests proved ruinous for the indigenous peoples.

Although Latin conquerors in the Mediterranean exploited subject peoples and territories as colonizers, they were also influenced by indigenous culture and civilization. This was particularly true where the prevailing culture was Byzantine, and thus regarded as prestigious by western conquerors. The Norman kings of Sicily employed Byzantine artists not only to beautify their churches, but also to make political statements about the sources and nature of their authority. Franks in the Crusader States and Cyprus patronized Byzantine mosaicists, painters and illuminators, and a hybrid school of crusader art, heavily influenced by Byzantine styles and techniques, developed as a consequence. The eastern Mediterranean, indeed, became a conduit that fed Byzantine styles and forms into the early Italian Renaissance.

Stimulation of Trade

Western expansion and settlement in the Mediterranean and northeastern Europe had important economic consequences. Before 1100 Italian commercial communities from Amalfi, Pisa, Genoa and Venice were already trading with North African and Levantine ports. After the establishment of the Crusader States, this trade increased dramatically, and the commercial interests of the Italian maritime cities went hand-in-hand with the political aspirations of the Latin settlers in the East. Possession of quarters in ports such as Acre, Beirut, Tyre and Antioch enabled western merchants to introduce luxury goods such as glassware, silks and spices to western markets.

This revival of long-distance trade around 1100 onwards in turn stimulated production in the West, in order to provide goods to sell in eastern markets. By 1300, the western nobility were conspicuous consumers of eastern goods, and the availability of what had once been luxuries came to be demanded by those who could afford them. Market forces had an effect on military and political policy, for by the 14th century papal demands for commercial embargoes on Muslim Egypt, in preparation for new crusades, were unpopular with states such as Venice, Naples and Aragon, which relied on the eastern Mediterranean trade. Venetian trade in the Black Sea in the 13th century, the result of their involvement in the Fourth Crusade, led to the opening up of new overland trade routes across Asia, pioneered by merchants such as the Polos. Commercial interests were also a strong element in the direction of the Baltic Crusades. Kings of Denmark and Sweden in the 13th century saw the Crusades as opportunities to open up and protect maritime trade routes to Riga, Estonia and Karelia.

Everywhere that the Latins settled – whether in the eastern Mediterranean, in Spain, in central and Eastern Europe or in the Celtic world – they were accompanied by the Church. Indeed, political control over newly-conquered regions

Mosaic of Christ at Monreale Monastery in Sicily. The vast mosaic of Christ against a gold background, with the Virgin and child below, dominates the church. The work of Byzantine and Venetian craftsmen in the late 12th century, the mosaic follows the Byzantine convention of depicting Christ holding scripture in one hand while the other is raised in blessing.

was often maintained through ecclesiastical institutions. The new monastic orders were instrumental in this process. For example, the Cistercians were prominent in frontier areas such as the German-conquered Baltic coast, Frankish Greece and the Scottish borders. In part, this was because they had by *c.* 1200 acquired a reputation for the efficient management of previously uncultivated land. However, the political angle was also significant: in Galloway, for example, bringing ecclesiastical reform to the 'barbarous' Scots went hand-in-hand with the extension of the king of Scots' influence over a previously ungovernable region.

The new orders of friars and the Military Orders also had a part to play in expansion: the Hospitaller, Templar and Teutonic Knights, obviously, in protecting conquered territory with their castles, while the Franciscans and Dominicans provided moral and spiritual support for the spread of Catholicism. A strong missionary element formed part of Latin expansion, particularly on the last pagan frontier in the Baltic, but also in the East. Regions that were already Christian, but regarded as out of step with Latin Catholic practice – such as Ireland, Wales and parts of Scotland in the 12th century, or Cyprus and the Byzantine empire in the 13th – were subjected to the influence of Latin bishops to bring them into conformity with Rome.

Accepting the Neighbours of Latin Christendom

In the wake of conquest, new attitudes emerged in Latin Christendom about non-Latins, whether Christian, pagan or Muslim. Celts were often seen as barbarous by virtue of their pastoral way of life, tribalism and legal traditions in which blood price and vendetta played a large part. Many of the same attributes identified in Gerald of Wales' critique of the Irish and Welsh in the late-12th century are also found in the description of Scandinavian and Baltic pagans by his contemporary Saxo Grammaticus. To the east, Greeks and Syrians were viewed with suspicion for allegedly being treacherous, incompetent in war and too fond of money, while, significantly, the Armenians, although suspect for similar reasons, were admired for their martial prowess. At the frontiers of Latin expansion, for example in Jerusalem, which attracted pilgrims from Ethiopia, the Caucasus and even India, western merchants, pilgrims and missionaries came across still more exotic peoples. In the 13th century, Latin rulers and popes came to regard the Mongols as potential allies against Islam. The Franciscan envoy William of Rubruck, while at the court of the Great Khan in Karakorum in 1253–54, took part in a religious debate with a Muslim, a Buddhist and a shaman. He found to his surprise that he had more in common with the Muslim than with the others. Growing knowledge of the wider world brought gradual acceptance, if not tolerance, of the neighbours of Latin Christendom.

The Byzantine Empire

The Byzantine empire was the successor state to the eastern half of the Roman empire. From its foundation by the emperor Constantine in the 320s, the political and cultural heart of the empire lay in the city of Constantinople.

"The [emperor's] throne was of immense size, made either of bronze or of wood. Lions covered with gold stood as if guarding it, and beating the ground with their tails, they produced a roar with mouths open and tongues moving."

Liutprand of Cremona, Antapodosis, translated by D.J. Geanakoplos, *Byzantium: Church, Society and Civilization Seen Through Contemporary Eyes* (Chicago University Press, 1984)

The Greek-speaking lands of the Balkans, Greece and Asia Minor provided the resources and manpower that enabled the empire to continue functioning in the East long after it had ceased in the West. The symbol of the empire was the imperial office itself. Emperors were considered to have been chosen by God and to represent divine majesty on Earth. A sophisticated and elaborate court ritual evolved to promote the image of the emperor; one western visitor to Constantinople in the 10th century described in amazement a device that lifted the throne to the ceiling so that the emperor could literally look down on his audience. Emperors were also considered to preside over the Orthodox Church, and to act as the guardians of Orthodoxy. Beneath the emperor a highly developed and literate bureaucracy governed the day-to-day affairs, using the Roman laws codified in the 6th century by Emperor Justinian. Armies were largely recruited from the estates of the great provincial aristocrats in Asia Minor, and it was the ability to tax these estates that maintained the imperial treasury.

Identity of an Empire

Byzantine identity was partly created by the empire's relationship to its neighbours and rivals. The Byzantines considered themselves as the continuation of the Roman empire, and therefore superior in status and heritage to other peoples, whether Christian, Islamic or pagan. The empire, however, had to withstand challenges to its domination from external powers and internal divisions. The east Roman provinces of Syria, Palestine and Egypt were lost to the Arabs in the 7th century, and Constantinople itself came under siege from the same enemy in the 670s. Revival under Leo the Isaurian (717–41) saw the establishment of Byzantine dominance in the eastern Mediterranean until the mid-11th century. However, the creation of a Bulgar state in the 8th century threatened Byzantine rule in the Balkans, while at the same time the Iconoclast controversy threatened the unity of Orthodoxy and caused social dissent in the empire.

The empire reached the height of its power and influence under Basil II 'the Bulgar-slayer' (976–1025), but after his dynasty foundered, the empire began to be overtaken by competitor states. The south Italian possessions were lost to the Normans and, more disastrously, Asia Minor to the Seljuk Turks in the 1070s. Although the Komnenos dynasty, particularly under Manuel (1142–80), succeeded in restoring a measure of influence throughout the Mediterranean, the empire could no longer recruit large enough armies to wield its

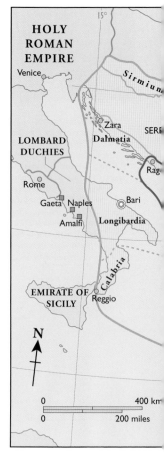

traditional authority, and the need to use mercenaries put an impossible strain on the treasury. In 1204 the Fourth Crusade, manipulated by the former Byzantine colony of Venice, was diverted to the conquest of Constantinople itself. Although the fragmented empire continued in exile in Nicaea until Michael VIII Palaeologus (1259–82) restored Constantinople itself, the 14th-century emperors ruled little more than the city and its immediate environs. By c. 1400 the Ottomans virtually surrounded the remnants of the empire, and the end, when it came in 1453, was long delayed.

A mosaic of Theodore Metochites and Christ in the Church of St. Saviour in Chora, Istanbul. The church is a masterpiece of Byzantine art. Metochites was a great scholar of the Palaeologan Renaissance.

Byzantine civilization and culture had an influence far beyond the reaches of the empire itself. Byzantine artistic styles and techniques were recognized as the benchmark of aesthetic taste and value throughout the Middle Ages, and Byzantine artists were employed by rulers from Damascus to Palermo. Although imbued with a sense of tradition, Byzantine culture was also capable of innovation, and some of its greatest treasures were produced during the 'Palaeologan Renaissance' of the 14th century.

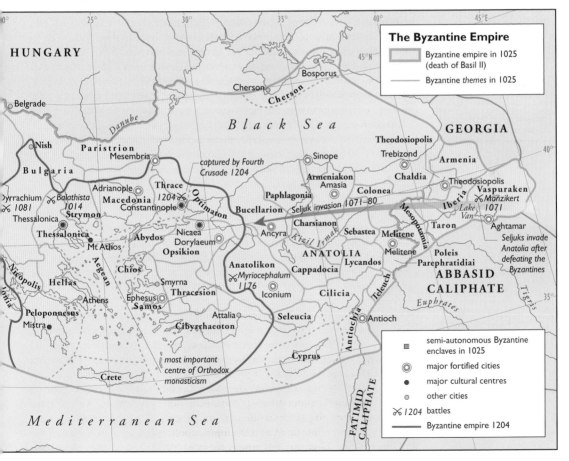

The Byzantine Empire

- Byzantine empire in 1025 (death of Basil II)
- Byzantine *themes* in 1025
- semi-autonomous Byzantine enclaves in 1025
- major fortified cities
- major cultural centres
- other cities
- ✕1204 battles
- Byzantine empire 1204

Kievan Russia

The first Russian principalities owed their existence to the trading routes and nascent political organization of the Vikings. When the Mongols invaded Kievan Russia in the 1230s, they found a complex mix of peoples with a rich culture and a prosperous economy.

"[Three brothers] built a town and named it Kiev after their oldest brother.... [Kii] was then the chief of his kin, and it is related what great honour he received from the emperor [of Constantinople] when he went to visit him."

The Russian Primary Chronicle

The remains of the great Golden Gates of Kiev in the Ukraine, built in 1037. Although the gates were destroyed during the Mongol raids, they were rebuilt in 1982.

The Varangians, a Viking clan, opened the earliest trade routes from the Baltic Sea east to Lake Ladoga, south along the Volkhov and Dnieper rivers to the Black Sea and then to the Byzantine empire. As they opened up each section of the new route, they established settlements and controlled the route first from Novgorod, then from Smolensk and finally, by 882, from Kiev. During the course of the 10th century the native Slavic peoples overthrew Varangian domination and set up a relatively centralized state which was run from Kiev by a new Russian dynasty. Prince Svyatoslav and his son Vladimir laid the foundations of the Russian state by organizing the Slavic princes of the region into a loose political confederation with the prince of Kiev at its head. The Russians were converted to orthodox Christianity through the Byzantine church during this period.

The Growth of Russian Power

Early dynastic dreams of Russian expansion were hampered by several obstacles. The geography of the area, with its marshy forests in the north and open steppes to the south, made domination of the entire north-south trade route to the Black Sea very difficult. Many tribes, with completely different ways of life, claimed sovereignty over various stretches of the route, and the south, with its open plains, was impossible to defend against the nomadic Turkic tribes from further east. First the Pechenegi and then the Cumans forced their way across the steppes and by 1054, after over 50 years of fruitless attempts to dominate the trade route south of Kiev, the Kievan dynasty lost control and Russian power shifted to the northern regions. Opportunistic expansionism from the West was also periodically a problem in the 13th century as wealthy Russian commercial centres were viewed covetously by German and Scandinavian traders.

The principalities of Novgorod, the largest Russian territory, and Vladimir-Suzdal became increasingly important after the fall of Kiev, although neither was able to achieve total domination of the Russian principalities. Russia's fundamental lack of political and cultural unity has never allowed more than brief periods of centralization, a fact noted by historians of all periods of Russian history. By 1200, with the southern steppes firmly controlled by the aggressive Cumans, the possibility of Russian expansion to the East was being explored. The Volga Bulgars, a Turkic subgroup, offered most resistance. Established since the 7th century in the area around the convergence of the Volga and Kama rivers, the Volga Bulgars maintained prosperous trading links with the Russians and the Byzantine empire and were keen to block a Russian advance across the Volga in order to preserve their monopoly on trade routes into Asia. Momentum for a Russian invasion increased during the opening decades of the 13th century, with Russian settlements such as Nizhniy Novgorod pushing eastwards into the frontier controlled by the Bulgars. In the end, encroachment was only halted by the devastation

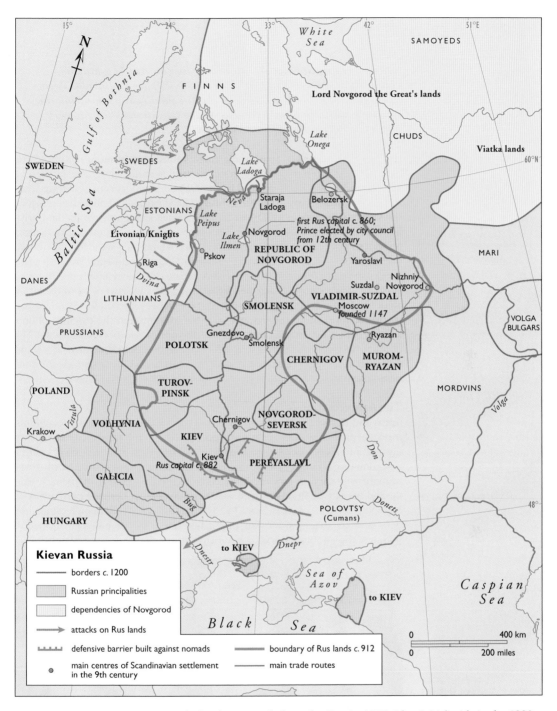

Kievan Russia

—— borders c. 1200

▨ Russian principalities

☐ dependencies of Novgorod

→ attacks on Rus lands

⊥⊥⊥⊥⊥ defensive barrier built against nomads

● main centres of Scandinavian settlement in the 9th century

—— boundary of Rus lands c. 912

—— main trade routes

0 — 400 km

0 — 200 miles

wrought by the Mongols from the East in 1237. After initial raids in the 1220s, the Mongols returned in full force in the 1230s to gain control of the wealthy Russian territories. By 1240 they had subdued most of the Russian principalities and even sacked Kiev. In the centuries that followed, the westernmost territories would yield to the Lithuanians and the Poles, while the eastern principalities would remain under Mongol control until a new Russian state, with Moscow as its centre, would emerge.

Moorish Spain

For nearly three centuries after their invasion in 711, Muslim conquerors occupied at least half of the Iberian Peninsula. Their presence in Spain lasted throughout the medieval period, and the resulting mixture of Islamic and native traditions shaped every aspect of developing Spanish culture.

"[On the door of a house in Andalus] every new king ... placed a padlock ... [King Roderick] refused saying, 'I will place nothing on it, until I know what is inside'; he ordered it to be opened ... inside were portraits of the Arabs, and a letter in which was written: 'When this door is opened, these people will invade this country.'"

History of the Conquest of Spain,
Ibn Abd-el-Hakem

The Visigothic rulers of Spain, their kingdom founded in the wake of the collapsing Roman empire, had only limited control over their subjects. Their fragile administration was easily crushed by the Arab and Berber armies entering Spain from North Africa early in the 8th century. The Umayyad Caliphate had replaced the Visigothic kingdom by 714, except for a small area governed by the Christian Asturians in the mountainous region of the northeast. Over the next 75 years Muslim forces pushed into Frankish territory where they were forcibly turned back, notably by Charles Martel at Poitiers in 732. Subsequently, Frankish plans for expansion beyond the Pyrenees were crushed at Roncesvalles in 778, when Charlemagne's army was defeated by Islamic forces who went on to recapture all of the Frankish king's gains south of the Pyrenees. By 900 the Asturians had recovered most of northern Spain from the Muslims and the essential boundaries between the Islamic and Christian territories had been established. The conflict between the two states, which were themselves divided at various times between regional princes, raged for centuries, with the struggle for domination favouring each side when the other faced internal difficulties.

The Arabicization of Spain

Arabs and Berbers settled in Spain, setting up local power bases. The administrative capital of Muslim Spain was Córdoba, by 900 the largest city in western Europe, and recognized by the Christian and Islamic worlds as a great cultural and commercial centre. Aside from their religion, the invaders from North Africa brought with them spices and fine silks from the East, their own culinary, artistic and literary traditions as well as a rich intellectual heritage particularly in medicine and the sciences. From 740 Syrian Muslims arrived in increasing numbers, and, as the new Muslim population mixed with indigenous Spanish peoples, the Moors emerged. Moorish culture married Arabian and North

The distinctive striped arches of the Great Mosque at Córdoba in Spain. The Arab arch comes from the Visigothic horseshoe arch which the Arab invaders used widely at Córdoba and are found in many mosques across the Muslim world. The horseshoe arch allows more height than the classical semi-circular arch, as well as better decorative use.

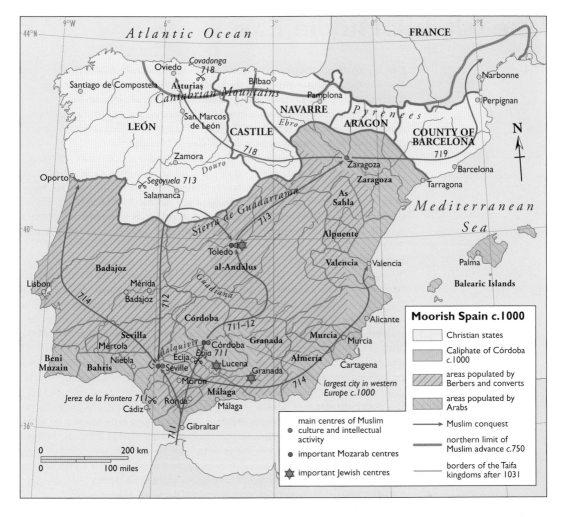

Moorish Spain c.1000

	Christian states
	Caliphate of Córdoba c.1000
	areas populated by Berbers and converts
	areas populated by Arabs

largest city in western Europe c.1000

- main centres of Muslim culture and intellectual activity
- important Mozarab centres
- important Jewish centres

→ Muslim conquest

— northern limit of Muslim advance c.750

— borders of the Taifa kingdoms after 1031

African Islamic traditions with local Iberian practices; the result was a rich and diverse hybrid with advanced learning and legal systems and refined literary and visual aesthetics. As well as threats from Christians to the north, the rulers of Muslim Spain faced internal political problems, often involving the status of local lords. Moorish rule and culture in Spain reached its height under Al-Mansur, chief minister of the Caliphate of Córdoba from 978 until 1002. Al-Mansur is remembered for his fostering of literature, learning and the arts.

The Christian population in Muslim-dominated areas began to absorb the new culture and become 'arabicized'. Christians were not generally forced to convert to Islam, although they were rewarded for doing so, but allegiance to the Muslim rulers was demanded. The exotic culture of their overlords began to affect the Christians, and the architectural motifs, liturgical developments and artistic traditions that arose among them are referred to as 'Mozarab', a term indicating the Christian culture which continued under Muslim rule. Mozarab influences are most apparent in art and architecture created for religious use, as it is here that Christian artisans were almost certainly at work. Illuminated manuscripts and liturgical metalwork provide the best examples of the style. Building by Christians was severely restricted within Moorish territory, and Mozarab architecture is most often found in reconquered Christian territories in northern Spain where it was transplanted by relocated mozarab clerics.

The Islamic Middle East

For the first century after the death of Muhammad, Islam was essentially Mediterranean in its political and cultural orientation. The capital of the Islamic world under the Umayyad caliphate (661–750) was Damascus, a city that had been part of the eastern Roman empire, and in which Byzantine craftsmen and artists were employed in the construction of the Great Mosque.

"The numerous suburbs [were] covered with parks, gardens, villas and beautiful promenades, and plentifully supplied with rich bazaars, and finely built mosques and baths.... Baghdad was a veritable City of Palaces, not made of stucco and mortar, but of marble."

Yakut,
Geographical Encyclopaedia

The Arabs absorbed and preserved Greek scholarship, developing a distinctive cultural synthesis that was recognizably Mediterranean. The tolerance shown to 'People of the Book' under Islamic rule in the Middle East enabled an Arabic-speaking class of Jews and Christians to reach positions of wealth and respect. Yet, tribal rivalries were never entirely suppressed within the 'House of Islam'.

Sunni and Shi'ite Split

During the 8th century the contest that had seen the Umayyads overpower the followers of Muhammad's son-in-law Ali in the 650s developed into a political and religious split between two branches of Islam, Sunni and Shi'ite. In 750 the Umayyads were defeated at Zab by Abu al-Abbas and the imposition of the new Abbasid dynasty heralded the first fragmentation of the Islamic world. An Umayyad, Abd al-Rahman, founded a breakaway caliphate in Spain in 756, which lasted until 1032, while in 789 the Magrib (Morocco) became independent of the Abbasid caliphate, followed in 800 by Ifriqiya (Algeria). However, the Abbasid foundation of a new capital at Baghdad on the Tigris in Mesopotamia (763), led to a new eastward orientation in the Islamic world, as the Arabs encountered and absorbed ancient Persian civilization, and began to exploit the silver resources of the Hindu Kush mountains. Baghdad, designed as a circular city surrounded by walls with over 300 towers, may have been the world's biggest city by the early 9th century. Its size and wealth reflected the height of Abbasid power under the caliph Harun al-Rashid (786–809), whose empire stretched from the Mediterranean to India. In the late-9th century, however, the Abbasid grip on the Islamic world began to wane again, and in 914 the Shi'ite Fatimid dynasty from Ifriqiya took control of Egypt. Worse fol-

The Wastani, or Dhafariya, Gate in Baghdad, Iraq. When Baghdad was built in 763 it was a circular city with defensive walls and gates. In 1203, under the Abbasid caliphate, a new wall with gates was built on the eastern side of the city and the Wastani is the only surviving gate from this period. Baghdad became a centre of knowledge in the medieval world.

lowed in 945 when Baghdad was captured by the Buwayhids, a Persian people. The Abbasid caliphate now became a spiritual office, while political control rested with the conquerors. Subsequent military dynasties competed for power in the eastern regions of the Islamic world during the 10th and 11th centuries until the arrival of the Seljuks from central Asia in the 1030s.

The eastward-looking direction of the Abbasids enabled them to absorb governmental and bureaucratic traditions from the Sasanian empire of Persia, and particularly in the reigns of al-Mansur, Harun al-Rashid and al-Ma'mun, great advances were made in the field of scientific knowledge. The court culture of Baghdad promoted an ostentatious luxury that promoted the image of an all-powerful caliphate. Despite the great personal wealth of the ruling dynasty, however, much of the government lay in the hands of the viziers, who were eventually to become virtually autonomous. Moreover, Abbasid rule was weakened by the recruitment of non-Arabs such as Turks and Berbers, many of whom were not Islamicized, into the caliphs' armies. During the 10th and 11th centuries Shi'ism developed serious challenges to the Sunni branches of law and religious thought. Nevertheless, it was also this period that saw the flourishing of Islamic culture through the work of philosophers such as al-Farabi (died 950) and literary figures such as al-Mutanabbi (died 965) and al-Isfahani. The new style of Arabic poetry, involving a greater use of metaphor and figurative language, developed a tradition of romance out of the much more austere norms of pre-Islamic Arabia.

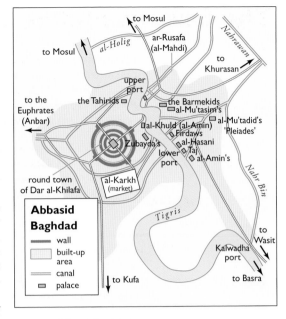

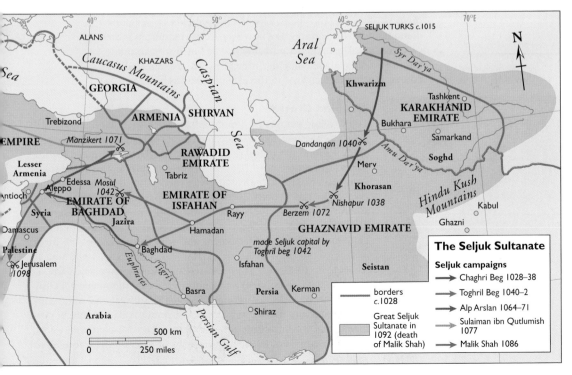

The Crusades to the Holy Land

The First Crusade, launched by Pope Urban II at the Council of Clermont in November 1095, was ostensibly a response by the knighthood and Church of western Christendom to an appeal for military aid from the Byzantine emperor Alexios Komnenos.

"If anyone desired to follow the Lord zealously, with a pure heart and mind, and wished faithfully to bear the cross after Him, he would no longer hesitate to take up the way to the Holy Sepulchre."

'Deeds of the Franks', The First Crusade: The Accounts of Eyewitnesses and Participants, August. C. Krey (1921)

A view of the Holy Sepulchre in Jerusalem during the Crusades from the Book of Hours of René, Duke of Anjou (1409–80).

The Seljuk invasion of Asia Minor in the 1070s had deprived the Byzantines of manpower and financial resources and cut the populations of Greek cities such as Antioch off from imperial rule. The Byzantines had traditionally employed western forces, particularly Normans and English, in their wars, and the emperor's request need have occasioned little surprise in the West.

The nature and course of the Crusade, however, owed more to conditions in the West than in the eastern Mediterranean. Urban II transformed the appeal for military aid into something quite different: an armed pilgrimage not simply for the restoration of Byzantine territory in Asia Minor, but for the recovery of the most important shrine in the Christian world, the Holy Sepulchre in Jerusalem. Where Alexios' appeal by itself might have given rise to a few thousand volunteers, the response to the general appeal made at Clermont and to the preaching across Europe was on a phenomenal scale, and when the crusaders first met a Turkish army they probably numbered about 100,000.

Crusaders were assured that their participation would obviate the need for penance for sins already committed. This was attractive to a knightly class otherwise confronted with the prospect of daunting penances that might jeopardize their livelihoods by either removing them from combat or forcing them to give up land in expensive endowments to religious communities. This is not to say, however, that crusading was an easy way out. Most knights probably had to find a sum amounting to several years' income in order to go on crusade; and, of course, it was a dangerous enterprise, with a low survival rate.

The First Crusade

The Crusade comprised a number of armies, each led by the feudal prince of a region: for instance, the counts of Flanders, Boulogne and Toulouse, and the dukes of Normandy and Lower Lorraine. Participants represented most regions of Western Europe, each loyal to its own leaders. That the Crusade was successful in its aim was due equally to the military prowess of the participants, the disunity among the heirs to the Seljuk empire in the east and a measure of luck. The crusaders took three major cities, Nicaea, Antioch (after an eight-month siege) and Jerusalem, and won battles against the Turks in Asia Minor at Dorylaeum in 1097, at Antioch in 1098 and at Ascalon in 1099. They suffered terrible privations, particularly at Antioch, and contemporary accounts of the expedition make it clear that it was regarded as having a peculiarly spiritual character, with processions and massed prayers before battle. A darker side of crusading zeal was manifested in massacres of Jewish communities by some crusaders en route, and by scenes of destruction at Jerusalem itself in 1099.

As a consequence of the First Crusade, new Christian states were established in the Levant: the Kingdom of Jerusalem, the Principality of Antioch, the County of Tripoli and the County of Edessa. A wave of emigration of knights, peasants and townspeople from the West sustained the survival of these states against almost continuous pressure from neighbouring powers until the fall of the Kingdom of Jerusalem in 1291. Successive crusades were subsequently launched to defend them and to recover the losses incurred, but of these only the Third Crusade (1189–92) regained substantial territory, and even that failed to recover the city of Jerusalem, which was lost to Saladin in 1187.

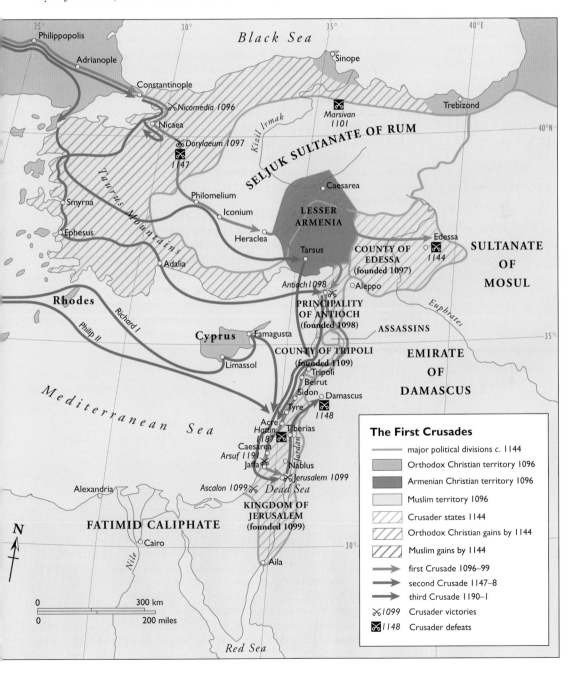

The First Crusades

———	major political divisions c. 1144
	Orthodox Christian territory 1096
	Armenian Christian territory 1096
	Muslim territory 1096
	Crusader states 1144
	Orthodox Christian gains by 1144
	Muslim gains by 1144
→	first Crusade 1096–99
→	second Crusade 1147–8
→	third Crusade 1190–1
✗1099	Crusader victories
✗1148	Crusader defeats

The Military Orders

The success of the First Crusade resulted in an increase in pilgrimage to the Holy Land. Unarmed pilgrims, however, were vulnerable to attack from bandits and marauders, and after one such massacre in 1119, a group of Frankish knights under the leadership of Hugh de Payen formed themselves into a religious order dedicated to the protection of pilgrims.

"They have now grown so great that ... about three hundred knights wear white mantles, in addition to the brothers, who are almost countless. There is not a province in the Christian world which has not bestowed [upon them] a portion of its goods .... Their wealth is equal to the treasures of kings."

William of Tyre, A History of Deeds Done Beyond the Sea

In the 1120s these knights – the Knights Templar, so called after the Temple in Jerusalem where they had their headquarters – began to recruit new members in the West. In 1129 they were formally recognized as an Order in the Church. The Templars combined two paths that the Church otherwise tried to keep distinct from one another: monasticism and knighthood. The treatise written to publicize their cause by Bernard of Clairvaux emphasized the hybrid nature of their profession. Although they took monastic vows and lived in communities like monks, the Templars were highly-trained fighting men, dedicated to the protection of the holy places under Christian rule. They prided themselves on their austerity and devotion, and the Order was run as a meritocracy in which all recruits, no matter how highly born, were equal.

The Hospitallers

The counterparts of the Templars, the Knights of the Hospital of St. John, began as carers for sick and dying pilgrims in the Holy Land. The Hospital itself had been founded before the First Crusade, but it attracted western donations and began to extend its operations throughout Europe from about 1110. The Hospitallers remained largely a charitable nursing institution until the 1130s, when they were given responsibility for garrisoning strategic castles in the Crusader States, the most famous of which was Krak des Chevaliers. By the 1160s, they, like the Templars, effectively formed a standing army that could be put at the disposal of the crown of Jerusalem. At their height, each Order could put about 300

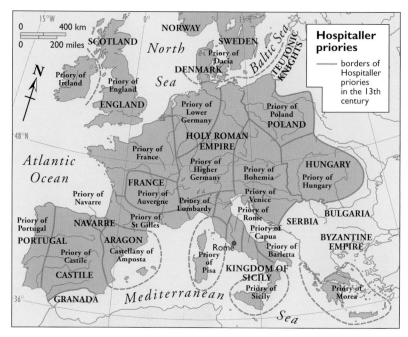

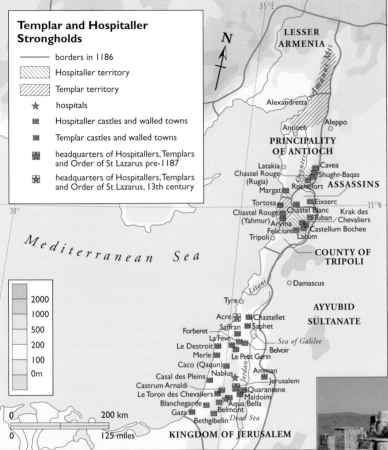

Templar and Hospitaller
Strongholds

— borders in 1186
▨ Hospitaller territory
▧ Templar territory
★ hospitals
🏰 Hospitaller castles and walled towns
🏰 Templar castles and walled towns
🏰 headquarters of Hospitallers, Templars and Order of St Lazarus pre-1187
★ headquarters of Hospitallers, Templars and Order of St Lazarus, 13th century

knights into the field, supported by thousands of men-at-arms. The success of the Templars and Hospitallers in the 12th century led to the creation of many smaller military orders; some, like the Teutonic Knights (1191), dominated by particular national groupings; others with a specific vocation, such as the Order of Lazarus devoted to the care of lepers.

The Military Orders, although based in the Crusader States, became wealthy and powerful as a result of patronage in the West. Like religious houses, they attracted bequests and donations from the laity; because these came mostly in the form of land, they became international land-owning corporations with property all over Christendom. Each Order had a complex internal structure of government, headed by a Grand Master, who was an internationally important figure. The Orders attracted men from the higher nobility as well as the knighthood: among early recruits to the Templars was the count of Champagne. The appeal of the Military Orders was much the same as the appeal of crusading, the chance to dedicate one's military calling to what was seen as the highest service of all. The Military Orders' influence and power waned in the East during the 13th century, as the Crusader States gave way to the Mamluks. In the early 14th century Philip IV of France brought charges of magic and heresy against the Templars, and the Order was suppressed by the papacy in 1314. The Hospitallers lived on, leading the resistance to the Ottomans in the Mediterranean, first from Rhodes and subsequently from Malta, while the Teutonic Knights devoted themselves to the German domination of the Baltic.

The fortress of Krak des Chevaliers in Syria. Initially built by Arabs, this mighty castle was turned into a crusader stronghold in the 12th century by the Hospitallers who controlled it for 127 years. Standing 650 meters (2130 feet) above sea level, the fortress dominated the pass that is Syria's gateway to the Mediterranean. Krak des Chevaliers was recaptured by the Mamluks in the late-13th century.

The Revival of Islamic Power

One reason for the success of the First Crusade was the absence of concerted resistance from the fragmented Islamic world. Individual rulers, such as Ridwan of Aleppo or Kilij Arslan in Asia Minor, opposed the crusaders only while they threatened their territory.

The Islamic world treated the crusaders simply as territorial competitors, and this failure to appreciate the spiritual significance of the Crusade was later seen by Muslim critics as indicative of a moral degeneracy within Islam. The first major blow against the new Crusader States was struck by Il-ghazi, who in 1119 defeated the Normans of Antioch at the Field of Blood, but he was unable to follow up his victory with the capture of Antioch itself. In the late 1120s, however, a more impressive figure, Zengi, atabeg of Mosul, emerged as the embodiment of a new spirit of jihad (holy war). Zengi's main ambition was domination over Syria, and his opponents were largely Muslim rivals. However, in 1144, he annexed the Frankish County of Edessa, an achievement for which he was lionized by contemporary religious scholars, whom he patronized. Zengi imported Iraqi religious educational traditions into Syria and began to develop an alliance between the Arab religious classes and the Seljuk military aristocracy that would underpin the revival of jihad ideals under his successors.

After his murder in 1146, Zengi was succeeded by his son Nur ad-Din. Nur achieved the unification of Syria in 1154 when the Damascenes, vulnerable to attack from the kingdom of Jerusalem, invited him to rule over them. Noted for his piety, Nur ad-Din promoted the image of the ideal Muslim ruler, devoting himself to maintaining Sunni orthodoxy in Syria. His building programme, which included the 'palace of justice' in Damascus, signalled an intent to oppose Shi'ism within his realms as well as to recapture Jerusalem.

Saladin

Nur ad-Din's biggest achievement was the annexation of Egypt and the suppression of the Fatimid caliphate in 1171. This was accomplished by his Kurdish protégé Saladin, who on Nur's death in 1174 was left in control of Egypt. Saladin usurped Nur's heir in Damascus and between 1174 and 1186 fought wars against the Zengid clan to capture Aleppo (1183) and Mosul (1186). Although during this period he sometimes, as in 1177 and 1183, threatened the kingdom of Jerusalem, Saladin was criticized by some contemporaries for his perceived pursuit of dynastic ambitions at the expense of Muslim rivals rather than of the jihad against the Frankish enemies.

Much of our knowledge of Saladin comes from his contemporary biographers, who portrayed him as an embodiment of the Muslim virtues of piety, generosity and zeal for the faith. To amass large enough forces to recapture Jerusalem from the Franks, Saladin first had to persuade the Islamic world that he was a legitimate jihad warrior. The coalition he put together for the invasion of the Frankish kingdom in 1187 comprised troops from as far afield as Yemen and Khorasan. With superior numbers and better strategic ability, he smashed the Franks at Hattin in July

An historiated initial showing Saladin campaigning in the Holy Land. In the late-12th century Saladin (1138–93) systematically won back Christian territory in Palestine for Islam. Saladin is one of the few historical figures from the period of the Crusades to have been viewed positively by both western and eastern sources.

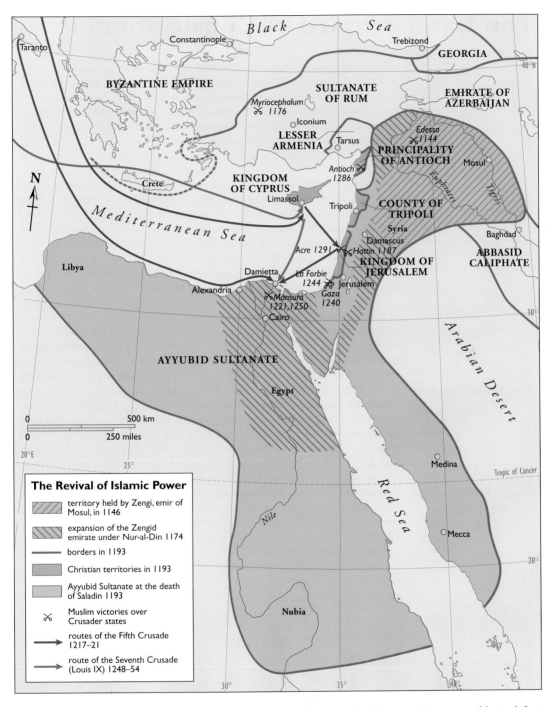

The Revival of Islamic Power

- ▨ territory held by Zengi, emir of Mosul, in 1146
- ▨ expansion of the Zengid emirate under Nur-al-Din 1174
- —— borders in 1193
- ▨ Christian territories in 1193
- ▨ Ayyubid Sultanate at the death of Saladin 1193
- ⚔ Muslim victories over Crusader states
- → routes of the Fifth Crusade 1217–21
- → route of the Seventh Crusade (Louis IX) 1248–54

1187 and captured Jerusalem that October. However, he was unable to defeat the kingdom entirely, and the Third Crusade (1189–92) won back some of his conquests. After Saladin's death in 1193 his brother al-Adil pursued a defensive policy towards the Franks that was largely copied by his successors until the Ayyubid dynasty was ended by the Mamluks in 1250. Saladin's true heir was Baibars, the Mamluk sultan of Egypt who in the 1260s returned to his aggressive jihad, and inflicted defeats on the Crusader States that proved to be fatal.

The Latin Empire of Constantinople

After the Fourth Crusade succeeded in conquering Constantinople in 1204, the crusaders who remained behind split up the newly-won lands between them. Since the emperor whom the crusaders had restored in 1203, Alexios IV, had been murdered by the Byzantines, a new Latin emperor, Baldwin, count of Flanders, was elected by the Venetian and Frankish crusaders.

> *"The emperor [Baldwin] told [his people] that he would not flee, and that they were to remain with him: [they say] never did any knight defend himself better.... On the field remained the emperor Baldwin ... and Count Louis; the emperor was taken alive and Count Louis was slain. "*
>
> Geoffrey de Villehardouin, *The Conquest of Constantinople*

The Venetians retained one-eighth of Constantinople, the Adriatic coast, the Ionian and Aegean islands and Crete, and established a colonial maritime empire. The emperor received the rest of the city of Constantinople, Thrace, the northwest region of Asia Minor and the islands of Chios, Lesbos and Samos. He soon found, however, that his was an empty title. Baldwin had little say in the distribution of fiefs, which meant that there was little reason for the new barons to be loyal to him. Central Greece and the Peloponnese were carved up between the Frankish crusaders, and eventually settled into the two main power bases of the Principality of Achaia and the Duchy of Athens.

Problems facing the Empire

From the start, the empire faced great problems. Conquering the city did not guarantee power over the empire. There were never enough knights, and emigration from the West never materialized. The empire was confronted by the two rival Byzantine successor states of Nicaea and Epiros, and by the Bulgar kingdom to the north. Baldwin was killed fighting the Bulgars in 1205, having refused to recognize their kingdom, and thus losing the chance of an alliance against the Byzantines. His successor, Henry II (1206–16), was more successful: his victory over Epiros in 1211 brought the Latin empire to the height of its power. But Thessalonika fell to Epiros in 1224, and in 1225 the Nicene emperor John III Vatatzes (1222–54) expelled the Franks from Asia Minor and almost reconquered Constantinople. Even the choice of the experienced John of Brienne as co-emperor in 1229 alongside the child Baldwin II (1228–61) proved futile. When John died in 1237, after a career that had included wearing the crown of Jerusalem, the empire had been reduced to the city of Constantinople. The city itself fell to the Nicene emperor Michael VIII Palaeologus in 1261, but by then the bankrupt Baldwin II had sold off everything of value, not only relics such as the crown of thorns, but even the lead from the palace roof.

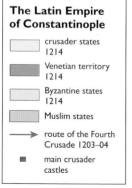

The Latin Empire of Constantinople

- crusader states 1214
- Venetian territory 1214
- Byzantine states 1214
- Muslim states
- → route of the Fourth Crusade 1203–04
- ⬛ main crusader castles

The wars that weakened the emperors in the north, however, protected the more remote Peloponnese, where the Villehardouins established the Principality of Achaia. In the mid-13th century they also became overlords of Negroponte, the duchy of Athens and the Archipelago, and were able to consolidate their feudal authority not only over their Frankish barons but also over the remaining Byzantine *archontes* (landowners), using French feudal customs enshrined in a written code of law. The principality eventually disintegrated under pressure from the Catalan Company (1311), a group of mercenaries from northern Spain. During its zenith under Geoffrey II (1229–46) and William II (1246–78), however, the Frankish court of Achaia enjoyed a reputation for chivalric culture. William II, who participated in Louis IX's crusade in Egypt (1249–50), built a palace at Mistra the grandeur of which can still be appreciated today.

The Latin empire, weak though it was, represented a vital component in the Crusader States. Popes recognized that the best hope for recovering the Holy Land lay in protecting the empire as a bridgehead to control the passage from West to East. However, although a crusade was launched against Nicaea (1237–39), and some individual rulers such as Charles of Anjou (1266–85) were prepared to invest in it, the cause of the Latin empire had little resonance among potential crusaders in the West.

The Palace of Despots at Mistra, near Sparta in Greece. William de Villehardouin established the headquarters of his Greek fief here after the Frankish conquest of the Peloponnese in 1205. Princes of the later Byzantine imperial family had the title 'Despot' and were based at Mistra. In its heyday under the Byzantine Greeks, Mistra was a centre of learning and the arts.

Below left: among the most famous items in the vast haul of treasures looted by Latin Christians from Constantinople after 1204 were the four huge bronze horses that still adorn the Basilica of St Mark in Venice.

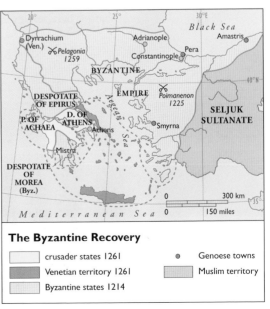

The Byzantine Recovery

crusader states 1261	● Genoese towns
Venetian territory 1261	Muslim territory
Byzantine states 1214	

The Baltic Crusades

"The gentiles are most wicked, but their land is the best, rich in meat, honey, corn and birds ... so most renowned Saxons, Franks, Lorrainers and Flemings, this is an occasion for you to save your souls and, if you wish, to acquire the best land on which to live."

The 'Magdeburg Appeal'

The Baltic Crusades began in 1147 as part of the Second Crusade (1147–48). In acknowledging that the conversion of the pagans of north-east Europe by force was as meritorious as the defence of the Holy Land and the Reconquista in Spain, Pope Eugenius III was simply recognizing German conquests that were already taking place, and giving them a religious justification.

The campaign of 1147–48 succeeded in enforcing the baptism of the Wendish prince Nyklot and his followers, but no widespread conversion actually followed. In 1172 Pope Alexander III once more recognized the war against Estonian and Finnish pagans as equal to that against Muslims. Absalom, bishop of Roskilde and Lund, was praised for his willingness to repulse the enemies of the faith as well as administer his bishoprics. Another justification, used to explain the campaigns of King Valdemar, was self-defence against Wendish raids on Danish shipping.

Commerce and Colonization

The German and Danish crusaders were more interested in commerce and colonization than in conversion. Danish kings saw the Crusades as a way of dominating the Baltic trade, while German crusaders wanted to settle new lands beyond imperial control. Neither could be accomplished by destroying the subject population that worked the land. Therefore in the 1160s Henry the Lion, duke of Saxony, used a puppet ruler, Pribislav, who had converted to Christianity, to rule the Wends, while King Valdemar, after conquering Pomerania in 1185, left the native prince of Riga in place as a tributary. Both missionary bishops and Christian rulers realized that the conversion of a pagan population was easier to accomplish if the local ruler of that population set the example. Once this happened, there was little incentive to undertake wholesale conversion.

Military Orders

Just as in the East, the Military Orders established a strong presence in the Baltic. Their role here, however, was to be far more controversial. The Teutonic Knights

The fortress of Marienburg at Malbork in Poland. Built in 1272, it was the headquarters of the Teutonic Knights who went to Poland in 1226 to help subdue and convert the Prussians.

were modelled on the Templars, but links to the German imperial throne drew them to Prussia and Livonia. From around 1250 onwards, they began to conquer new lands there, sometimes in competition with two local Orders – the Sword Brothers of Riga, founded in 1202, and the Knights of Dobrin, founded by a Cistercian bishop in 1206. The Sword Brothers had a reputation for extreme violence: in 1205–06 a peaceful attempt to convert the Livonians by performing a miracle play failed when the natives were terrified by the realism of the 'Massacre of the Innocents' scene. In the end they kidnapped a papal legate who had recommended their suppression to the Pope. The Sword Brothers joined the Teutonic Order in 1236.

By 1292, Latin control in the Baltic extended 300 miles east of Gdansk, and comprised something reaching a million new inhabitants. The Livonians, who had been tributaries of the Lithuanians and the Russians of Novgorod, were conquered by Albert, the third bishop of Buxtehode, and his Sword Brothers. The mission to the Prussians, started around 1200, had been completely accomplished by the Teutonic Knights by c. 1272.

Meanwhile, the Danish king Valdemar II (1202–41) conquered Estonia. Unlike German expansion, Danish expeditions were controlled by the crown, and conquests treated as economic investments. There was little Danish settlement, and the purpose of Danish involvement was to secure trading privileges so as to control the supply of furs, amber and timber from the north-east.

Swedish Campaigns

The same was true of Swedish raiding in the eastern Baltic. Although the Swedes did settle in western Finland, further east they encountered the entrenched interests of the Russian state of Novgorod. In 1240 Alexander Nevsky (1220–63) defeated a Swedish crusade on the Neva River, near present-day St. Petersburg, thus acquiring his surname. Swedish kings had little inclination to occupy land that was barren and frozen for the greater part of the year. Nonetheless popes were prepared to treat Swedish economic wars as crusades because they defended Latin interests against the Orthodox Russians.

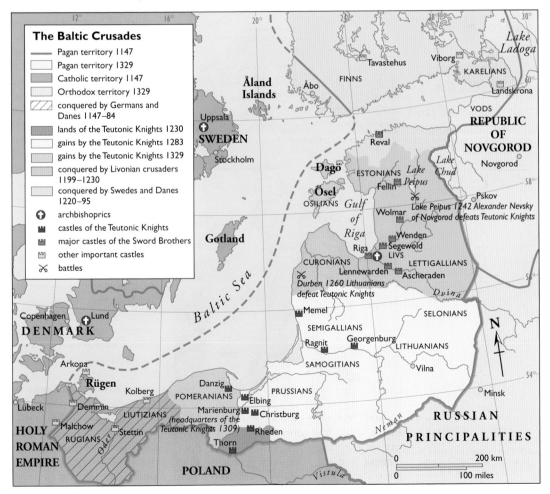

The Baltic Crusades

- Pagan territory 1147
- Pagan territory 1329
- Catholic territory 1147
- Orthodox territory 1329
- conquered by Germans and Danes 1147–84
- lands of the Teutonic Knights 1230
- gains by the Teutonic Knights 1283
- gains by the Teutonic Knights 1329
- conquered by Livonian crusaders 1199–1230
- conquered by Swedes and Danes 1220–95
- ☧ archbishoprics
- ♜ castles of the Teutonic Knights
- ♜ major castles of the Sword Brothers
- ♜ other important castles
- ✕ battles

The Reconquest of Spain

"And great was the rejoicing in the city that did reign,

When the lord Cid took Valencia and within the town had won,

For himself the Cid Rodrigo took the fifth part of all,

And coined marks thirty thousand unto his share did fall."

The Lay of the Cid, Semicentennial Publications of the University of California: 1868–1918

Although intermittent warfare between the Christian and Muslim powers in the Iberian Peninsula began soon after the Arab invasion of the early 8th century, properly speaking the term 'Reconquista' applies to the period from the mid-11th century onwards.

The event that precipitated this phase of conflict was the fall of the caliphate of Córdoba in 1032 and the consequent fragmentation of political power among the Muslim successor states, known as 'taifas'. In the mid-11th century, most of Spain came under the rule of the taifas. Although the Christian states of the north were smaller than the taifas, they exercised an influence out of all proportion with their populations and size. Largely rural states governed by a military aristocracy much like that in the rest of Europe, the Christian kingdoms developed a powerful knightly class with expansionist tendencies.

The Castilians

By 1054, the early hegemony among the Christians of Navarre under Sancho Garcia III (1000–35) had given way to that of the kingdom of Léon-Castile, united by his son Fernando I. In 1063 Fernando's raid into al-Andalus induced the taifas of Seville and Badajoz to begin paying him tributes ('parias'). Such payments not only enhanced his reputation but also his capacity to enlarge his army and dominate his neighbours still further. In 1074, his successor Alfonso VI enjoyed an annual income of 74,000 dinars from parias, incomparably more than could ever have been acquired from taxation of his subjects or the income from the crown estates. Castilian supremacy among the Christian states was assured by Alfonso's conquest of Toledo in 1085, which also demonstrated how a strong ruler could redistribute the taifas among competing leaders.

Problems over succession in the early 12th century allowed Aragon to make ground in the race for new lands, and under Alfonso I 'the Battler' (1104–34) it more than doubled its size, notably with the conquest of the taifa of Zaragoza in 1119. In the 1130s, dynastic union with Catalonia resulted in a strong rival to Léon-Castile in the north east. In the west, a

A portrait of Alfonso VI of Castile (1040–1109). This comes from a 12th-century compilation held in the archive of the cathedral at Santiago de Compostela in Spain. Alfonso VI drew Spain nearer to the papacy and the French while remaining open to Arab influence.

descendant of Alfonso VI of Castile created the kingdom of Portugal, enhanced by the capture of Lisbon in 1147 as part of the Second Crusade. The taifa states were weakened not only by their military weakness in the face of aggression, but also by the North African Murabit regime, which they called on for help in the late 11th century, and its successor dynasty, the Almohads, in the 12th. The decisive encounter in the Reconquista was the Christian victory at Las Navas de Tolosa (1212), in which the Christian states combined forces with French knights. Although the taifa of Granada fell only in 1492 to the joint forces of Aragon-Castile, its power had progressively diminished during the 14th century.

The Reconquista was until the early 12th century largely a war of territorial conquest waged by a rural and militaristic society against a more prosperous urban one. The career of El Cid, a Castilian baron who, after being banished by Alfonso VI, served the taifa of Zaragoza before setting up as a mercenary captain on his own, demonstrates that the primary incentive was money rather than religion. Religious ideals, however, began to infiltrate across the Pyrenees, particularly after the First Crusade to the East, with the arrival of French knights. The popularity of pilgrimage to Santiago de Compostela brought Spain into a wider cultural orbit, and from the 12th century new conquests were accompanied by the imposition of Roman religious forms in place of the native Mozarab rites that had grown up among Christians who had lived under Arab rule.

Europe and the Mongols

The rise of the Mongol empire in the 13th century would permanently alter the political and social demographics of Europe and Asia. Asia, both east and west, suffered the worst of their aggression but Europe, particularly Hungary, Poland and the Russian principalities, also fell victim to their devastating raids.

"While the King was in Cyprus, the great Khan of the Mongols sent envoys to him, greeting him courteously, and announcing that the Khan ... was ready to help him conquer the Holy Land and deliver Jerusalem from the Saracens. The King received them with great favour, and ... sent back ... his own envoys. "

John de Joinville, *Life of Saint Louis*

The Mongols were a nomadic people originating in the area of Asia now known as Mongolia. They consisted of disparate clans and were only united in the early 13th century under Temujin, who was, in 1206, renamed Chingis ('universal') Khan in honour of his accomplishment. By his death in 1227, Chingis Khan had built an empire stretching from the Pacific Ocean west to the Caspian Sea, and from the Kunlun mountains above Tibet north to the Irtysh River in Russian Siberia. Chingis Khan divided his empire among his four sons, with Ogedai elected as the next Great Khan.

Expansion of the Empire

Under Ogedai and his successors, Güyük and Möngke, the empire continued to expand; the Jin empire in northern China fell in 1234, the Mongols invaded the Tibetan plateau and, to the west, Iran, Iraq, Syria, Georgia and the Turkish Sultanate of Rum collapsed under the fierce Mongol assault. Europe was threatened by the Mongols not just along the southern borders of the Byzantine empire, but also north of the Black Sea where they had conquered the Volga Bulgars and entered the Russian principalities. Moscow was sacked during the Mongol invasion of 1237–40; Kiev was razed in 1240 and it was from there that the Mongols launched their campaign into Poland and Hungary, defeating large European armies at Legnica and Mohi in 1241. The Great Khan Ogedai died in December 1241 and the Mongols appear to have pulled back out of Europe.

From this point the Mongols focused on their East Asian territories, never entering Europe again, and by the middle of the 13th century, the Mongol stranglehold on western Asia had also begun to loosen. Despite several khans who continued to exhibit a taste for territorial expansion, notably Kublai (died 1294) in China, and Timur the Lame (died 1405) whose empire, based in Samarkand, stretched from Delhi to Baghdad, what little unity that the Mongol empire had

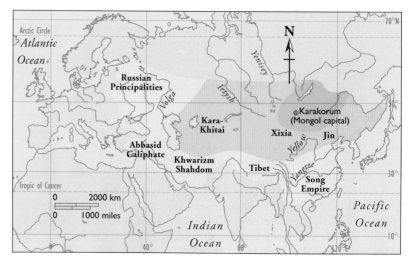

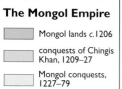

The Mongol Empire

Mongol lands c.1206

conquests of Chingis Khan, 1209–27

Mongol conquests, 1227–79

enjoyed was lost following the death of the Great Khan Möngke in 1259.

The impact of the Mongol invasions of Europe is hard to assess. Only the Russian principalities could be said to have suffered directly over a lengthy period. The rest of eastern and central Europe certainly felt the immediate destruction wrought by the Mongols, who preferred devastation to diplomacy, but the hasty retreat of the Mongols in 1241 ended any long-term threats, although Europeans continued to fear the legendary warriors. The Mongols would have been unlikely to dominate Europe for long in any case as the forested and relatively densely-populated areas of Europe would not have been suitable for them to manoeuvre their large cavalries or graze their mounts. Perhaps the most important repercussions for Europe involved the Mongol domination of western Asia, especially the areas formerly under Turkish control. The Mongol link with the

The Gur-Emir (Grave of the Emir) mausoleum in Samarkand, Uzbekistan. The mausoleum, one of the most important monuments of Islamic art, was built in 1404 for Timur the Lame's favourite grandson.

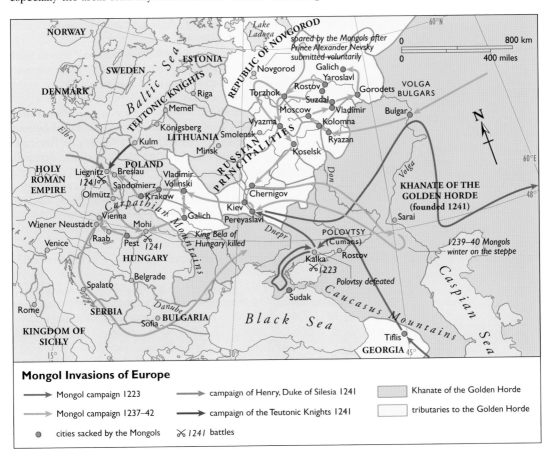

Mongol Invasions of Europe

→ Mongol campaign 1223	→ campaign of Henry, Duke of Silesia 1241	▨ Khanate of the Golden Horde
→ Mongol campaign 1237–42	→ campaign of the Teutonic Knights 1241	▢ tributaries to the Golden Horde
● cities sacked by the Mongols	⚔ 1241 battles	

Turks began early in the 13th century when Chingis Khan strengthened his armies by the addition of Turkish warriors, allowing Turkish culture and dialects to spread across his empire. The rise of the Ottomans, who went on to occupy much of southern Central Europe from the late 15th century, was a direct result of the toppling of the Seljuk Sultanate of Rum by the Mongols.

Part IV: The Later Middle Ages

If the period c. 1000–1300 was characterized by the fast pace of expansion and innovation in European political, social and cultural institutions, the later Middle Ages was a period of slower development. By 1300, the institutions that would largely continue to govern European society well into the modern period were already in place, while the social and economic trends that would bring about more profound change in the 16th and 17th centuries were just beginning to take effect.

Politically the period from *c.* 1300 to *c.* 1500 saw the further strengthening of monarchies across Europe, a trend accompanied by a clearer sense of national and racial identity. Kingship, already the normative form of government in most of Europe, became increasingly articulate and bureaucratic, while at the same time associated more closely with the governance of sovereign territories fixed by treaty. Although the influence of the Church within national frontiers was no less important than in earlier periods, the international authority of the papacy waned, and by around 1500 it was arguably as low as at any time since the start of the reform movement of the 11th century.

Similarly, the Holy Roman empire, which had been pre-eminent among secular authorities before the mid-13th century, largely because of its special relationship with the papacy, went into a serious and irreversible decline in the later Middle Ages. Emperors found the expectations, responsibilities and aspirations that went with their title unwieldy and burdensome in an age dominated by national kingships. The most eloquent testimony to this shift in the balance of forces is the fate of late medieval Italy. For so long caught between the competing ambitions of imperial and papal authority, Italy, once both had declined, slipped into political chaos in the 14th and 15th centuries. In both Italy and Germany, the political fragmentation that lasted until the 19th century was the legacy of the early medieval papal-imperial axis and of the political philosophy inherited from the Roman empire.

New Political Philosophy

The period *c.* 1300–1500 saw the rise of a political society with distinctive theories and laws that had evolved from the practical experience of rulership rather than from the hierocratic political philosophy of the later Roman empire. This is reflected in some of the literary and cultural products of the period, from Dante's *On Monarchy* (*c.* 1313), a polemic against papal claims to secular authority, and Marsilio of Padua's *Defender of the Peace* (1320–24), which sought to establish a balance between the spiritual and the secular in society, to the allegorical fresco cycle by the Lorenzetti brothers, *On Good and Bad Government*, painted for the municipal government of Siena in the 1320s. Similarly, contesting royal governments promoted historical views of their authority that married literary invention with perceived claims to the antiquity of 'national' crowns: for example, the defence of English claims to the throne of Scotland in the 1290s and the Scottish Declaration of Arbroath (1320).

One characteristic of later medieval political society was its internationalism. After the death of Emperor Frederick II in 1250, the papacy dealt with the claims of the Hohenstaufen heirs by inviting first the English, then the French ruling dynasty to rule the kingdom of Sicily. Charles I of Anjou, the younger brother of Louis IX of France, successfully defeated Frederick's son Manfred (1266) and grandson Conradin (1268) to conquer Sicily, but Angevin rule was

Illustration of King Edward III (1312–77) paying homage to Philip VI of France in 1329. Edward was required to pay personal homage to the French king for his inheritance of the duchy of Aquitaine. This act, which affirmed Philip's authority while invalidating Edward's claim to the French throne, was resented by the English king and laid the political seeds for the Hundred Years War (1337–1453) between France and England.

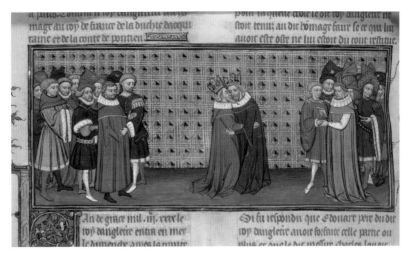

fatally wounded by the 'Sicilian Vespers' (1272), a rebellion fomented among the Greek-speaking population of the island by the Byzantine emperor. The ultimate beneficiary was the kingdom of Aragon, which, through its conquest of the Balearics and increasing trade in the eastern Mediterranean, was becoming a significant power. A divided kingdom resulted: Sicily was ruled by an Aragonese dynasty and Naples (comprising the mainland part of the old kingdom of Sicily) by the Angevins.

The attempted conquest of one national territory by another was also a feature of later medieval political society. Thus the Hundred Years War between England and France, unlike previous conflicts between English and French kings in the 12th and 13th centuries, arose from a claim to the throne of France by Edward III, rather than from rights stemming from territorial lordships within the French kingdom. This development was, of course, one consequence of intermarriage among European ruling dynasties, which produced a royal class with international links and thus, sometimes, dynastic claims that crossed national frontiers. Just as the English kings had plausible claims to the French crown, the Aragonese ruled Sicily and the French Naples, so also a cadet branch of the French dynasty became kings of Hungary, and a French noble family, the Lusignans, continued to rule Cyprus until 1475. A further consequence of this tendency for domestic political society was the distancing of royal families from the nobility. This was particularly noticeable in England. Whereas in the 12th century, Anglo-Norman nobles fought in defence of family possessions on both sides of the English Channel, by the end of the 13th century English barons were out of sympathy with Edward I's attempts to consolidate his power in Gascony. The pursuit of English royal claims in France in the 14th and 15th centuries, therefore, had either to be presented to the barons as opportunities for personal enrichment, or seen by them as necessary to national interests. The latter, of course, presupposed that the baronage now thought in such terms.

France and the Monarchy

It is testament to the growing strength of royal governments that the Hundred Years War, while hugely destructive to property and rural populations, did not produce the same kind of political vacuum in France as did the chronic warfare that dominated 14th-century Italy. Despite the capture of one king (John II) and the insanity of another (Charles VI), the French monarchy survived and by the mid-15th century had driven the English from France. By the 1480s, largely through the efforts of Louis XI (1461–83), it had also succeeded in dominating

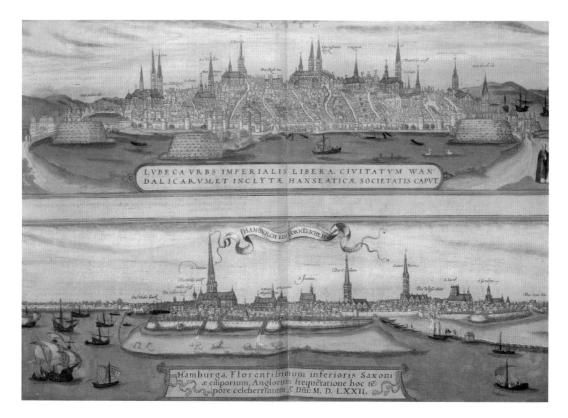

LVBECA VRBS IMPERIALIS LIBERA. CIVITATVM WAN-
DALICARVM.ET INCLYTÆ HANSEATICÆ SOCIETATIS CAPVT

HAMBVRCH EIN KORNÊLICHE HA

Hamburga. Florentissimum inferioris Saxoni
æ emporium, Anglorum frequêtatione hoc tê
pore celeberrimum. Dñi. M. D. LXXII.

A map of Lübeck and Hamburg from *Civitates Orbis Terrarum* edited by Georg Braun (1541–1622) and engraved by Frans Hogenberg (1535–90). The *Civitates* is a fascinating collection of city plans, views and maps from all over the world which provides a unique view of urban life at the turn of the 16th century.

the powerful duchy of Burgundy, whose independence from the crown under a succession of powerful dukes (1361–1477), coupled with possession of the wealthy county of Flanders, made it a dangerous rival.

The French crown under Philip IV 'the Fair' (1285–1314) had developed increasingly effective mechanisms for raising taxes and ensuring that royal rights were recognized throughout France. As in England, increased use of the law and legal professionals as advisors to the crown was critical to this process. Although kings could not afford to disregard the higher nobility in their advisory role or to alienate them to the point where they would no longer support them in 'national' military adventures, they tended to rely for day-to-day governance and the enactment of policy on a professional body of bureaucrats and lawyers trained in the universities. Practical government originated from the royal household, rather than from kings in consultation with their nobility. As governmental bureaucracies became increasingly complex, kings tended to remain centred in capital cities rather than itinerant. This led to the development of royal courts as places where patronage, justice and government were negotiated in the presence of the king. One function of the nobility and of an increasingly well-defined class of 'gentry' throughout Europe was to approve and grant taxation. Without taxes, kings could count only on the income of crown lands, which was never sufficient, but in order to obtain consent for taxation, kings had to persuade their nobility that they would also benefit.

Despite increasingly sophisticated governmental methods, monarchies were still vulnerable, particularly in the face of war and when the reigning monarch pushed the baronage too far, as happened in England under Richard II (1377–99), who was deposed, or proved incompetent to rule, as was the case with Charles VI of France (1380–1422) and Henry VI of England (1422–61). England's huge investment in the Hundred Years War was frittered away by military failure in the 15th century, and by the 1450s great barons were able to raise private armies and flout royal authority. Yet the damaging dynastic conflict that ensued, the Wars of the Roses, resulted in a still stronger crown with more centralized powers by the end of the century.

Chivalry and the Crusades

The growth of national sentiment did not obstruct the continuing development of an international noble class. Chivalry was by the 14th and 15th centuries largely a cultural construct, perpetuated in self-consciously anachronistic works of literature glorifying historical and mythical figures such as Charlemagne and Arthur. Yet as an ideal it proved resistant to political realities, as for example in an episode described by the chronicler of the Hundred Years War, Jean Froissart. In his account, French knights fearful of being captured by English archers were relieved to recognize among a group of English knights some with whom they had served on campaign with the Teutonic Knights in Lithuania. Ties of friendship among the self-selecting aristocratic class, fostered by periodic service for the Cross, overrode national quarrels between kings. The cause of the Crusades endured despite the loss of the Holy Land in 1291, and proved a touchstone of chivalric virtue for the knighthood. When no crusade against the Turks or the Moors in Spain was imminent, knights could take service with the Teutonic Knights for a season. The political value of crusading for the upper nobility lay in the prestige it conferred: thus, at the 'Feast of the Pheasant' in 1454, the Duke of Burgundy displayed his wealth and independence with a ritual vow to lead a crusade against the Turks.

Class

Class consciousness was, if anything, more marked in the later Middle Ages than before. A degree of social mobility was possible during a period of territorial expansion and new settlement, but by around 1300 opportunities for autonomous military adventuring were restricted. The natural disasters that visited Europe in the 14th century – for example, the widespread failure of harvests that led to famine in France in the 1320s, or, worse still, the successive outbreaks of plague that peaked in the Black Death (1347–53) – exacerbated class conflict. Shortage of labour as a result of the plague in which a third of the population may have died meant that landowners who could not afford to lose labour became more restrictive in the application of feudal services over their peasants. Those who were able to escape such services, particularly skilled labourers, found the market in their favour, but the widespread sumptuary laws passed to prevent the lower classes from adopting the dress of their superiors shows how fearful governments and the nobility were of social mobility.

The walled garden of the Palazzo Medici-Riccardo in Florence, Italy. The mosaic pavement is decorated with the Medici coat of arms. The Medicis were one of the most powerful and wealthy families in Florence. They were part of the patrician class, rather than the nobility, and were regarded throughout their history as friends of the common people.

In England and France the wealthy and powerful had good reason to fear mob violence, as demonstrated during the Jacquerie in France in 1358 and the Peasants' Revolt in England in 1381. The immediate causes of these uprisings may have differed, but the general context was similar: the common people felt unfairly burdened by the expenses of war falling on top of the regular impositions of outdated feudal dues. The destructive effects of chronic warfare added considerably to the burdens of the economically underprivileged. In both

John Lydgate and the Canterbury pilgrims from an illustrated manuscript of *The Siege of Thebes* by poet John Lydgate (1370–1450). In *The Siege of Thebes* Lydgate wrote himself into Chaucer's *Canterbury Tales,* which tells the stories of a group of pilgrims travelling to Canterbury. Chaucer and Lydgate were part of the movement in the 14th century that saw a burgeoning of vernacular literature.

France and Italy, mercenary companies damaged local economies through widespread looting and arbitrary seizure of goods.

The Black Death

It is difficult to evaluate, but impossible to overstate, the effects of the Black Death. Dramatic architectural examples, such as the dismembered walls of the planned new cathedral in Siena, completed eventually on a much smaller scale because of the shortage of labour, serve as reminders of how European society retrenched in the face of mass death. It has long been argued by historians of later medieval culture that a pervasive sense of pessimism and scepticism is noticeable after the Black Death in art and literature. A marked preoccupation with death and dying became one of the chief characteristics of late medieval arts. The wealthy paid for ever more elaborate tombs whose decoration graphically contrasted worldly pleasure with the indignity of death. Chantry chapels, founded specifically to employ priests to say Masses for the souls of the benefactors' families, became widespread. Whether connected with the Black Death or as a separate development, the nature of late medieval spirituality saw subtle but profound changes. One of these was an increase in the range of private devotions, seen for example in the proliferation of Books of Hours commissioned by the nobility and middle classes. This coincided with a growing rise in literacy among the laity, and therefore an interest in what individuals could do for their own salvation. Book ownership became less and less restricted to the higher nobility, particularly after the invention of moveable type and mass printing in the 15th century. When books became affordable, they were no longer symbolic objects of power confined to the clerical elite. But in order to be able to sell books to a larger market, printers had to have a wider variety of reading matter to print. The rise of vernacular literature all over Europe, exemplified by poets such as Dante in Florence and Chaucer in England, was an important development in the growing self-consciousness of secular and lay culture.

Dissatisfaction with the Church

In part, this self-awareness may have arisen from growing discontent with the Church, although not with Christianity itself. Attacks on papal wealth and power were widespread in the 14th century. The Italian humanist scholar Petrarch, who famously described the papal presence in Avignon as the 'Babylonian Captivity' of the Church, was objecting to the perceived self-indulgence and pursuit of temporal power by popes. In fact, the Avignon popes were as a whole neither more nor less worldly than their immediate predecessors, and the choice of Avignon made pragmatic sense given the political chaos in 14th-century Italy. But the papacy had begun to lose respect from the 1260s onward, when a succession of mediocre popes easily dominated by the French crown appeared to follow policies centred on the pursuit of power rather than the values of the Gospel. Internal dissension, such as the persecution of the Spiritual Franciscans and other groups that advocated the literal observance of poverty by friars, from the 1290s to 1330s, did not help the public image of the papacy. Indeed, dissatisfaction with the established Church was apparent in heretical movements in the 14th century, particularly the Lollards in England and the Hussites in Bohemia, while in the 15th century the Brethren of the Common Life and similar groups promoted radical reforming ideals based on communal penance and lay-centred spirituality. The Lollards, followers of the Oxford theologian John Wyclif (died 1384), denied the doctrine of transubstantiation and rejected papal headship of the Church, pilgrimages and the cult of saints. Religious dissent could provide an impetus for other forms of rebellion, which was why it was feared by both Church and state. Not all the criticism, however, came from heretics: during the 15th century in particular, humanist influences, originating in Italy, sought to purify some of the perceived excesses in the Church. The keynote of reform was to return to some notion of the 'primitive' Church. Alongside high-minded dissatisfaction, however, conventional late medieval spirituality remained vibrant, and it would be a mistake to assume that the Reformation of the 16th century was an inevitable consequence of dissent.

Culture in the Later Middle Ages

Cultural life in the later Middle Ages, which with the perspective of hindsight can appear to have been little more than a prelude to the Italian Renaissance, was in fact neither stagnant nor parochial. The Renaissance did not burst unannounced on to the scene as a new phenomenon, but emerged as the product of an evolving European culture out of a combination of internal developments and external influences. The external influences can be seen most clearly in the relationship between Byzantine culture and the West. Long exposure to Byzantine arts in the Crusader States, and through the Latin occupation of the Byzantine empire in the 13th century, had brought new artistic techniques such as panel painting, which derived from Byzantine icons, to Italy. Artists such as Duccio, Cimabue and Giotto in the late 13th and early 14th centuries were already exhibiting Byzantine influences in form and style. The heirs of these painters were Masaccio, Fra Angelico and others experimenting with perspective in the early 15th century. Artists needed patrons, and Italy, with its highly-fragmented political fabric, provided courts, such as that of the Medici in Florence or the Sforza in Milan, who competed with one another for cultural prestige as well as power. These courts also patronized a humanistic literary, philosophical and historical culture that took its inspiration from Byzantine exiles in the 15th century. The revival of classical philosophy was based on a revival of classical Latin and Greek language, rather than the over-complex theological Latin of the universities. Renaissance culture, indeed, marked the triumph of courts and lay patronage over the Church-dominated universities.

The 15th century also saw another stage in the expansion of Europe's horizons. The voyages of discovery undertaken by the Portuguese were primarily intended to open up new trade routes. While the Portuguese took the lead in discoveries in Africa, the Spanish were at the end of the century promoting voyages to the New World. Due to Christopher Columbus' famous voyage, 1492 has often been taken as a symbolic date for the start of the modern era. Columbus, however, was looking for a maritime route to the spice-rich East Indies, which was a traditional medieval aspiration. Moreover, if we are looking for symbolism, 1492 also serves as the climax of another medieval practice that had become traditional, crusade and conquest. In the same year that Columbus landed in the Caribbean, the united kingdoms of Castile and Aragon completed the Reconquista of Spain by conquering the Moorish kingdom of Granada. This was followed shortly afterwards by the expulsion of the Jews from Spain, and thus the end of the most prosperous, creative and sophisticated Jewish community of Europe. The modern European world therefore began with the culmination of medieval ideals and practices.

The Hundred Years War

Disputes over English sovereignty within France led to the Hundred Years War between France and England. By the mid-1330s open hostility existed between the two nations, and until France defeated England in 1453, control of various regions changed hands regularly.

"In these masculine garments ... I have been sent by God to ... help Charles, the true king of France, and to place him on his throne from which the English king and the duke of Burgundy strive to chase him."

Joan of Arc, as quoted in Johann Nider's 'Formicarius', written between 1431 and 1438

Most English territories in France had been seized by Philip Augustus just after 1200; Gascony remained the most important English possession, although the English gained Ponthieu, in northeastern France, in 1279 through Eleanor of Castile, wife of Edward I. Much of Edward's reign was spent attempting to subjugate Scotland and Wales, but his position as a vassal of the French king (for Gascony) and a Franco-Scottish alliance against him in the 1290s led to several years of warfare between England and France. Following his ascent to the French throne when Charles IV died heirless in 1328, Philip of Valois began raiding England's south coast and attempted to seize the English-held duchy of Guyenne. Edward III of England, himself a claimant to the French throne through his mother, Isabella of France, retaliated by declaring himself king of

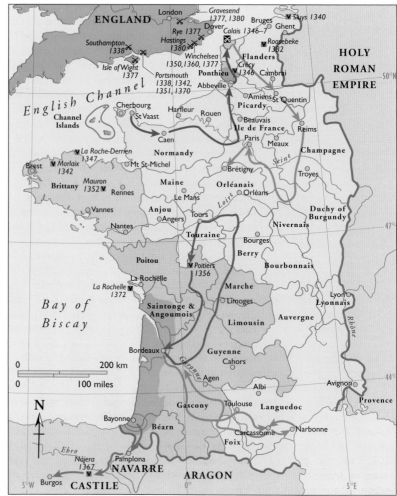

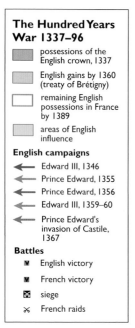

The Hundred Years War 1337–96

- possessions of the English crown, 1337
- English gains by 1360 (treaty of Brétigny)
- remaining English possessions in France by 1389
- areas of English influence

English campaigns

- ← Edward III, 1346
- ← Prince Edward, 1355
- ← Prince Edward, 1356
- ← Edward III, 1359–60
- ← Prince Edward's invasion of Castile, 1367

Battles

- ▼ English victory
- ▼ French victory
- ✕ siege
- ✗ French raids

France and defeating the French fleet at Sluys (1340). This first phase of the war lasted until the peace of Brétigny (1360), when Edward forfeited his claim to the French throne, his newly-conquered lands north of Paris, and the French king John II whom the English had captured at the battle of Poitiers (1356) in return for increased lands in southwestern France and a large ransom payment. Numerous English victories, such as the famous battle of Crécy (1346), characterized the French military campaigns of Edward III and his son Edward, the Black Prince, although the French were far from subdued, and the Scots continued to plague England from the north.

English Victory at Agincourt

By 1369 the French had regrouped and seized most of England's recently acquired territories, as well as renewing their naval assault along the English coast. The Franco-Scottish alliance, serious financial problems and the Peasants' Revolt of 1381 were among the factors weakening England's defences and it is largely due to the deteriorating mental state of the French king Charles VI, rather than to any effective English resistance, that a truce was again declared in 1396. This was short-lived; by 1400 a new campaign under the English Lancastrian kings, Henry IV and Henry V, was underway. France was weak, its monarch mentally unstable and two factions, the Burgundians and Armagnacs, fighting to obtain political control. The brilliant English victory under Henry V at Agincourt (1415) and his recapture of Normandy by 1419 meant that once again England appeared in ascendancy.

Under the treaty of Troyes (1420) Burgundy became England's ally and recognized Henry V as heir to the French throne. Henry's death in 1422 caused minimal upset as the English army in France continued to advance southwards. With assistance from Burgundy (which also controlled Flanders), the English weakened the Franco-Scottish alliance with victories against both countries, and in December 1431 Henry VI of England was crowned king of France in Paris. French resistance was, at this point, rather underestimated by the English; the Dauphin Charles had himself been crowned king already in 1429, following the raising of the English siege of Orléans by the French army with the help of the young Joan of Arc. In 1444, with the Burgundians now allying themselves with the French, the English were forced to accept another truce, but this time the French had the upper hand. English momentum was never regained and, lacking finances and dependable allies, the English saw Normandy fall in 1450 and Gascony the following year. The French finally defeated the English at the battle of Castillon in 1453. With the port of Calais England's only remaining territory, Charles VII could now claim undisputed sovereignty over France.

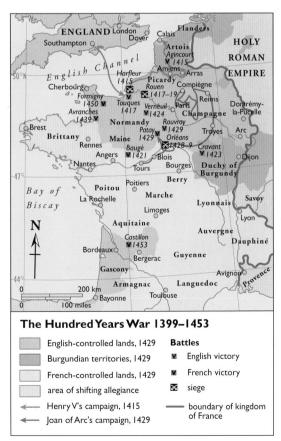

Portrait of John II the Good, King of France (1350–64) by an unknown French artist. John the Good was defeated and captured by the English at Poitiers in 1356 and imprisoned in England during the first phase of the Hundred Years War.

The Hundred Years War 1399–1453

English-controlled lands, 1429	**Battles**	
Burgundian territories, 1429	◪	English victory
French-controlled lands, 1429	◪	French victory
area of shifting allegiance	◩	siege
← Henry V's campaign, 1415	—	boundary of kingdom of France
← Joan of Arc's campaign, 1429		

The Black Death

"The Florentines walked about carrying ... flowers or fragrant herbs ... because everywhere the air seemed full of the stench emitted by the dead and dying."

Giovanni Boccaccio, the *Decameron*

A deadly plague, known as the Black Death, arrived from Asia in 1347 and rapidly spread throughout Europe from Mediterranean trading ports. Within two years most of Europe had been affected, and by the late-14th century the total population had decreased by as much as one third.

The plague was not new to Europe or Asia; regular outbreaks occurred throughout antiquity, and continued into the modern period until improved hygiene and the development of antibiotics rendered epidemics less likely. The Black Death of 1347–53 was on a larger scale than anything previously witnessed by Europeans, and the fear and confusion surrounding outbreaks of the disease rapidly turned to panic and chaos before an inexplicable phenomenon which could wipe out whole families and villages in a matter of days. There were two strains of the Black Death, both transmitted by infected fleas carried by rodents. Both bubonic plague, which attacks the lymphatic system, and pneumonic plague, which involves the lungs, nearly always proved fatal, but pneumonic plague was more severe, often resulting in violent death within a day or two of contraction. Most cases seem to have been bubonic with symptoms including high temperature, vomiting, swelling in the armpits and groin and delirium.

The Spread of Plague

Already rampant throughout eastern Asia, the plague entered Europe when Cuman warriors from the steppes south of Kiev catapulted corpses of plague victims over the walls of a Genoese trading post in Crimea which they held under siege. From here the disease spread to other European trading centres, first around the Mediterranean, by 1348 throughout the Balkans, Italy, most of France and eastern Spain, and continuing north and eastwards until, by the early 1350s, it travelled back into Asia via Scandinavia and the Russian principalities.

Generally the cities and towns were harder hit than the countryside because the poor sanitation and cramped living quarters in urban areas allowed greater ease of cross-infection. The isolated nature of a rural village, however, meant that one infected person fleeing a nearby city could single-handedly spread the disease among the local population in only a matter of days. Different regions of Europe suffered greater fatalities

Illustration of Death strangling a victim of the Black Death, from the Stiny Codex. The Black Death occurred at a bad time for Europe, which was already suffering from the effects of a flagging economy, famine and the Hundred Years War. Subsequently a tone of despair and morbidity filtered into the art of the 14th century.

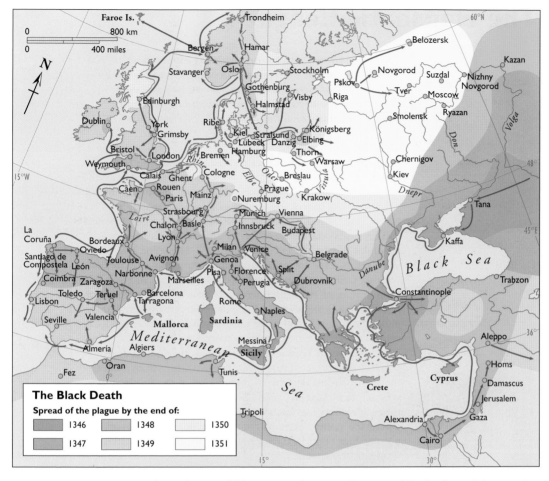

The Black Death

Spread of the plague by the end of:

1346	1348	1350
1347	1349	1351

than others, with Tuscany, southwestern France and England sustaining massive losses, while Flanders, Poland and the eastern Holy Roman empire remained relatively unaffected.

The impact of the Black Death on European society was profound. Its arrival in the late 1340s followed a long period of dramatic social and cultural change. Most of Europe was experiencing general economic instability (as financial institutions struggled to adapt to the sudden upsurge in international trading and the corresponding demands of currency-based commerce), as well as social upheaval between urban and rural dwellers, and between monarchs and baronial landowners. Previous minor outbreaks of plague and regular crop failures and famine also proved problematic. After the plague abated, the social and economic systems were even more tenuous. Artisans within cities were in great demand and could charge much higher prices, thus putting pressure on the already overstretched merchant classes to reinvigorate industrial and trading mechanisms which were in total disarray. The countryside was equally short of workers, and landowners now needed to find large sums of cash to pay their workers reasonable wages or risk grave shortages of food and related products such as wool. The ruling classes had watched kings, barons, and bishops fall victim to the plague, leaving a political landscape also in need of regeneration. The Black Death permanently changed the social balance in Europe, loosening economic and social control by the aristocracy and paving the way for improved conditions for the workers.

The Hanseatic League

German expansion into the Baltic region in the 12th and 13th centuries stimulated overseas trade between the peoples of northern Europe. By 1250 German commercial centres had begun to band together to form a mutually beneficial business partnership known as the Hanseatic League.

> *"A fine of 50 marks will be imposed on any German who enters into ... a trading partnership with Russians or who accepts goods from them as commission. The same will be imposed on anyone entering into partnership or accepting commissions for handling Italian, Flemish, or English commodities. "*
>
> Legislation set by the Hanseatic *Kontor* of Novgorod, *c.* 1295

Derived from the German term *Hanse*, or guild, the Hanseatic League at its height in the 14th century stretched across northern Europe from Novgorod to Edinburgh and numbered around 100 members. Lübeck, refounded as a German trading post by Henry I the Lion of Saxony in 1158, served as the geographical and organizational centre of the group, whose members operated under the 'law of Lübeck' from 1265. Hanseatic law codes were set in place to regularize trading throughout the region, with set tariffs and recognized business practices, and to guard the interests of Hanseatic merchants against those of local or regional political powers. As a powerful quasi-political trade guild, the league could close ranks against unreasonable local rulers or even, in extreme circumstances, declare war.

The Hanseatic League also researched and produced navigational charts and acted to protect Hanseatic ships from pirates in the North and Baltic Seas. Its domination of the northern seas was unquestioned between the mid-13th and late-15th centuries. Members met each other occasionally to air grievances and review policy decisions, but on the whole individual trading partnerships controlled their own affairs within the established Hanseatic framework.

The *Kontore*

Most northern German cities quickly joined the Hanseatic traders, followed by trading posts along the Baltic sea where merchants from Germany had settled, including Gdansk, Riga and Revel (modern Tallinn). Although the association consisted primarily of commercial centres under German control, early on the Hanseatic League established foreign depots, or *Kontore*, to monitor trading practices abroad and to control imports and exports with traders from outside the Hanseatic region. The four initial *Kontore* were in Novgorod, Bergen, Bruges and London, and they primarily traded furs, timber and fish, cloth and wool respectively. Grain, salt, copper and tin were also among the numerous commodities traded between the Hanseatic cities as well as between the league and its trading partners from Italy and the Mediterranean. Visby, on Gotland, served as the centre for Baltic overseas trade, with Bruges serving as the main North Sea Hanseatic port; trade between northern and southern Europe took place primarily at the great fairs, such as those in Antwerp, Geneva and Lyons. Trade routes into Asia which could supply silks and spices for the luxury market were jealously

A miniature of Hanseatic ships in 15th-century Hamburg from the Hamburger Stadtrecht (charter of Hamburg). Hamburg's proximity to the main trade routes of the North and Baltic Seas made it one of the important ports of northern Europe.

The map shows the Hanseatic League trade network across northern Europe, with scale bar 0–400 km / 0–200 miles.

Labels include: Trondheim, Bergen, NORWAY, Oslo, Stockholm, Reval, Novgorod, Lake Ladoga, Shetland Islands, Orkney Islands, Tartu, Pskov, REPUBLIC OF NOVGOROD, Visby, Gotland, Riga, Polotsk, Vitebsk, SWEDEN, Baltic Sea, TEUTONIC KNIGHTS, Smolensk, SCOTLAND, Edinburgh, North Sea, DENMARK, Malmö, Falsterbo, Kovno, Königsberg, LITHUANIA, Newcastle, York, Hull, Lübeck: capital of the Hanseatic League, Stralsund, Danzig, Elbing, ENGLAND, Boston, Groningen, Rostock, Wismar, Stettin, Thorn, RUSSIAN PRINCIPALITIES, Kiev, King's Lynn, Yarmouth, Kampen, Hamburg, Lüneburg, Bremen, Berlin, Ipswich, Deventer, Osnabrück, Brunswick, Frankfurt an der Oder, POLAND, Lublin, Bristol, Damme, Soest, Magdeburg, Dnepr, London, Dortmund, Goslar, Bruges, Antwerp, Leipzig, Breslau, Lemberg, Cologne, Erfurt, Frankfurt am Main, HOLY ROMAN EMPIRE, Prague, Krakow, Rouen, Nuremberg, Paris, Linz, Strasbourg, Augsburg, Buda, FRANCE, Geneva, Lyon, Milan, Venice, VENICE, Bordeaux, (to ENGLAND), Genoa, PAPAL STATES, Nice, ANDORRA, Marseilles, GENOA, Rhône, Loire, Rhine, Elbe, Oder, Dvina.

The Hanseatic League

○ major member of the Hanseatic League
○ minor member of the Hanseatic League
● Wendish and Pomeranian circle
● Saxony, Thuringia and Brandenburg circle
● Prussia, Livonia and Sweden circle
● Rhine-Westphalia and Netherlands circle
▪ Kontore
○ other cities
—— trade routes

guarded and, although they were initially controlled by Venice and Genoa, the Hanseatic League soon established its own connections with Asian traders via Prague and their *Kontore* in the Russian principalities.

Competition between rival trading centres, which had developed initially because of the protection offered by the Hanseatic League, began to weaken the German trading confederation in the later Middle Ages. England and Flanders forged their own trading agreements centred around the cloth industry. The Scandinavians developed stronger local sympathies and set up their own commercial partnership, as did many of the Slavic peoples, such as the Poles and Lithuanians who joined forces in 1397. Novgorod ceased to be a Hanseatic *Kontor* in 1494. The 15th century also saw the development of the great maritime trading nations, among them Portugal, England and the Netherlands, whose exploration and colonization would open trading possibilities undreamt of by most medieval merchants. By the early 15th century Hanseatic domination was weakening, but the league continued into the 17th century, having served as an important model for numerous larger and more extensive trading concerns.

Disaffection with the Papacy

The Pope and his curia left Rome for Avignon in 1309. By 1377, when the papal entourage returned to Rome, the election of a second pope at Avignon led to the Great Schism of the Catholic Church. Europe became more and more factional as rulers pledged allegiance to one pope or the other, and only at the council of Constance (1414–17) was the Church reunited under a single leader.

"Now I live in France, the Babylon of the West. ... Here reign the successors of the poor Galilean fishermen who have forgotten their origin. I am astounded ... to see luxurious palaces and fortified castles, instead of an overturned boat for shelter."

A letter from the Italian poet Petrarch to a friend, mid-14th century

Rome was not a safe place for much of the medieval period; wealthy Roman families jockeyed for political power and control of the papacy, and Rome's position as the centre of western Christianity made it very appealing to foreign invaders. Clement V, a Frenchman and the subject of intense pressure from King Philip IV of France, took up official residence in Avignon, which belonged to the king of Naples, a papal vassal.

All seven of the Avignon popes were Frenchmen, as were most cardinals created in the 14th century, and French influence on the Church was at its height during this period. However, rifts within Europe opened as other powers strove to counter what they saw as undue French control over the papacy; in particular the Holy Roman emperors felt keenly the physical removal of the Pope from the Italian peninsula to a location surrounded by French territory. The most beneficial aspect of the move to Avignon was the reorganization and streamlining of papal bureaucracy, which in turn stimulated broader ecclesiastical

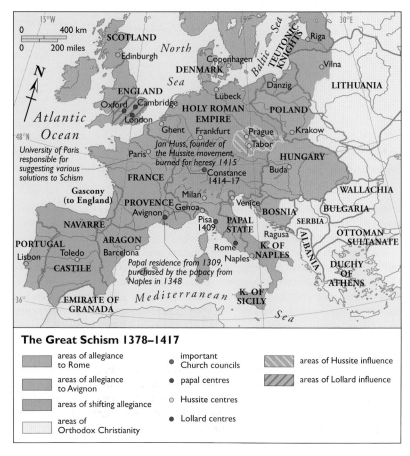

The Great Schism 1378–1417

- areas of allegiance to Rome
- areas of allegiance to Avignon
- areas of shifting allegiance
- areas of Orthodox Christianity
- important Church councils
- papal centres
- Hussite centres
- Lollard centres
- areas of Hussite influence
- areas of Lollard influence

reform. The financial machinery of the papacy, which funded the entire western Church as well as the papacy itself, was also made much more efficient, but the increased financial rewards were quickly eaten into by the lavish lifestyle at the new papal court.

At the same time the College of Cardinals was developing into a powerful contingent within the Church. As overseers of the machinery of papal affairs, the cardinals can be seen as the driving force behind many of the papal initiatives of the period. Pope Gregory XI, the last Avignon pope, finally realized the professed dream of his immediate predecessors and returned to Rome in January 1377, only to die in March 1378. The Italians, led by Florentine dissidents, demanded an Italian successor in response to the French domination of the Avignon popes and the College of Cardinals. The cardinals, mostly Frenchmen forced to react to local pressures within Rome, duly elected Pope Urban VI, archbishop of Bari, who then adopted strict reforms to curb the extravagance of the papal court. The cardinals countered by electing an antipope, the Frenchman Clement VII, who established himself in Avignon. For nearly 20 years papal prerogative was to remain split between Rome and Avignon, but by the 1390s external pressure was mounting for a reconciliation.

View of the entrance to the Palace des Papes in Avignon, France. Avignon became the headquarters of a group of cardinals in the late-14th century who came close to destroying papal authority in Rome. The palace was constructed by the third Avignon pope, Benedict XII (1334–42), and there the Avignon antipopes held extravagant court from 1378 until the election of Pope Martin V in 1417 when the papacy regained its position.

The secular powers of Europe, led by France, agreed to unite behind a single legitimate pope, and when both popes refused to make way for a new replacement, the College of Cardinals called the council of Pisa in 1408 where they voted to realign the two factions behind their newly elected pope, Alexander V. The cardinals deposed the two reigning popes, declaring that a conciliar decree superceded papal authority. The situation worsened, with three reigning popes until the council of Constance was called in 1414. It closed in 1417 after the deposition of two popes and the abdication of the third; under Martin V the papacy was restored to its former position as the single office at the head of the Church. The papacy, after years of extravagance and corruption, was in disarray. The Sacred College of Cardinals, on the other hand, had consolidated its power and established conciliarism, the authority of the council over that of the Pope, as a guiding principle within the Church.

Italy at the Beginning of the Renaissance

The later Middle Ages was a period of intense political change and cultural development within Italy. The Italian peninsula was dominated by powerful secular communes with expansionist tendencies. The Church played a fairly minor political role, although its importance as a patron of the arts, and increasingly as a diplomatic power broker, resurfaced by the late-15th century. A revival of classical culture from the mid-14th century heralded the end of the Middle Ages and the dawn of the Renaissance.

"There remained many examples of ancient buildings, temples and theatres, from which ... much could be learned; ... I visited and examined all of the ancient ruins I could, no matter how unimportant, to learn what I could from them."

Leon Battista Alberti,
On Architecture,
Book VI, Chapter II

In Italy political power was synonymous with territorial aggression from the late 14th century and the major players, concentrated in northern and central Italy, were Milan, Venice and Florence. The papal states, welded together so carefully by medieval popes wary of invasion by neighbouring rulers, collapsed in the wake of the Avignon Papacy and the Great Schism, and, to the south, Naples and the kingdom of Sicily were controlled by the kingdom of Aragon until the end of the 15th century.

Milan, Venice and Florence

Milan enjoyed the initial period of ascendancy in the years following the Black Death. Under Gian Galeazzo Visconti, Milan expanded its power base throughout the Piedmont and Emilia, as well as east into the Veneto and far enough south to threaten the sovereignty of Florence. Although much of this territory was lost following the death of Gian Galeazzo in 1447, Milan, under the Sforza dukes, emerged as a great cultural and artistic centre. The republic of Venice, with its long established monopoly on trade with the East, began a campaign of expansion on the Italian mainland in order to protect its trade routes through Lombardy and over the Alps from Milanese aggression. This move proved very beneficial to the republic as it largely prevented encroachment by Milan, and allowed Venice to maintain its revenues as Venetian colonies in the eastern Mediterranean came under threat from the advancing Ottoman Turks. Venice, always a wealthy and culturally refined city, continued its long tradition of artistic patronage up to and beyond the end of the Middle Ages. Florence grew, in the 15th century, from a locally powerful city-state to a regional political force whose cultural tastes played a crucial role in Renaissance ideals. Allied first with Venice and later with Milan, Florence was governed by the Albizzi from 1382 until 1434, when Cosimo the Elder, the first of the Medici rulers, assumed control. Cosimo was instrumental in drafting the peace of Lodi (1454), through which an alliance was forged between Florence, Venice, Milan, Naples and the papacy against any threat to the balance of power in Italy; 50 years of peace and prosperity followed this agreement. The 1490s brought an end to political stability in Italy; in 1494 the French king Charles VIII entered Italy to take up

Filippo Brunelleschi's great dome at the cathedral of Santa Maria del Fiore in Florence. Completed in 1436, the dome – the largest ever constructed in bricks and mortar – is one of the outstanding achievements of Renaissance architecture. Its size reflected Florentine determination to excel in all things.

Italy at the Beginning of the Renaissance

- —— borders *c.* 1450
- —— border of the Holy Roman Empire
- Papal states
- Venetian lands
- Genoese lands
- Aragonese empire in Italy

- ● cities with populations over 50,000
- ◉ cities with populations 25,000–75,000
- ▣ important centres of Renaissance culture
- ★ important 15th-century secular courts
- ■ Italian University cities (by *c.*1430)
- △ Medici bank branches
- ▲ cities with elected governments

his claim to the throne of the kingdom of Naples. The league of Venice was quickly formed by Milan, the Holy Roman empire, Naples and the papacy, and Charles withdrew. His departure left Italy disorganized and politically weakened, with the great powers left to rebuild their former power bases.

Florence, under the Medici, became a great centre of learning and the arts based on ancient Greek and Roman ideals, a cultural phenomenon known as Italian Humanism. Genuine historical interest existed alongside the Medici's masterful use of artistic patronage as propaganda, and soon Florence abounded with architectural and artistic commissions recalling the glory of the ancient Romans, yet inextricably linked to Medici influence and funding. From Florence these new cultural ideals spread, with regional variations, throughout Italy, even taking root within the papal court in Rome.

The Ottoman Invasion of Europe

The core of the Ottoman empire before 1500 included the Turkish heartland in Anatolia and the Balkan region of eastern Europe. The Ottoman Turks pushed northwards into Europe as far as Vienna in the 16th century, and their official domination of Anatolia, the Middle East and Egypt would continue until 1922.

"15 June 1389. There was a battle between the Bosnians and the Great Turk.... The emperor Murad (I) was killed as was the king of Bosnia (the Despot Lazar). Because of the great losses neither the Turks nor the Bosnians gained the victory. And the battle was on Kosovo Polje."

Entry for the battle of Kosovo from the *Annales of Ragusa*

Named for their ruler Osman I, the Ottoman Turks were one of numerous clans of Turkmen nomads forced into Anatolia as the Mongols pushed westwards across Asia in the 13th century. From their base in Bursa (captured in 1324), the Ottomans, with their fervent commitment to the expansion of Islam, conquered northwestern Anatolia by 1345 and began their advance into Europe with the capture of Gallipoli in 1354. Under Orhan, son of Osman, links were forged with the crumbling Byzantine empire which was forced to allow Ottoman raiding parties into the Balkan region. In 1361, under Murad I, the Ottomans took Adrianople, which they renamed Edirne and established as their capital city. The Byzantine emperor John V was forced to become a vassal of Murad in 1371 as Turkish armies streamed through his territories and into the Balkans. Murad I was killed in 1389 at the battle of Kosovo when an alliance of Balkan peoples fought unsuccessfully to stop Ottoman aggression in the region.

Period of Consolidation

The reign of Bayezid I lasted only 12 years, but it was during this period that Ottoman power and lands were consolidated. In the Balkans, Bulgaria was conquered and Wallachia and Serbia forced to accept Ottoman overlords; a European crusade against the Turks culminated in decisive victory for Bayezid's forces at the battle of Nicopolis in 1396. Nearly all of Anatolia was also brought under Bayezid's control for a short period before the Mongol leader Timur the Lame captured him in 1402 at the battle of Ankara. Murad II, grandson of Bayezid, reestablished Ottoman control in Anatolia and entered into armed conflict with Hungary and Venice. He formed a new power base among his recently conquered subjects to counter the threat to his leadership by older Turkish families who had strongly supported his ancestors. These new subjects were often Christian converts to Islam and in return for gifts of lands they supported the sultan and provided men for his elite army, the Janissary. The *devshirmeh*

View of the Muradiye Camii and graveyard at Bursa in Turkey. The Muradiye Camii, constructed by Sultan Murad II between 1424–26, is a complex located in the city centre which includes a mosque, theology school and royal cemetery. The Orhan mosque is one of the most important structures of the early Ottoman period.

system, where young men from the Balkans were forced to convert to Islam and rigorously trained, provided him with further loyal soldiers and servants.

Mehmed II the Conqueror was the last great Ottoman sultan of the 15th century; his reign saw the fall of Constantinople, the extension of Ottoman lands within the Balkans to the Hungarian border and south through Greece into Morea, and the consolidation of control in Anatolia and Ottoman encroachment into the Crimea. Following Mehmed's death in 1481, the pace of Ottoman expansion slowed and internal problems plagued the empire. By the accession of Suleiman I the Magnificent in 1520, however, Syria and Egypt had been conquered and the Ottoman empire entered into its greatest phase. The first 200 years of the Ottoman empire saw the development of a complex machinery of government as the empire grew in size. At first regional political structures and ruling families were often left in place (in exchange for vows of allegiance and hefty tributes); cultural and religious institutions were also left intact. Over time the Ottomans initiated a more centralized system to enforce control and to secure revenue collection over large areas. Ottoman culture became more refined and began to spread, although over Ottoman territories in Europe this imported culture enriched rather than replaced indigenous traditions.

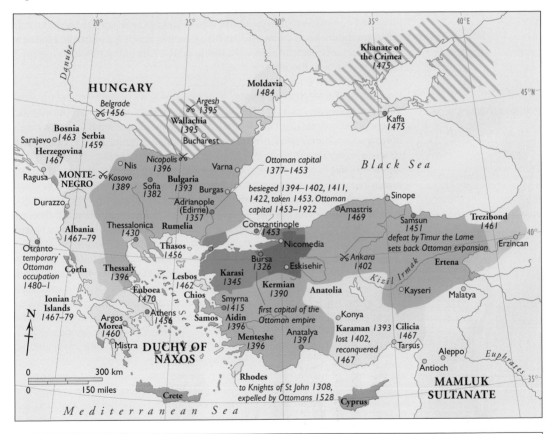

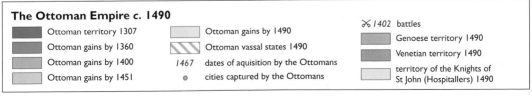

The Ottoman Empire c. 1490

- Ottoman territory 1307
- Ottoman gains by 1360
- Ottoman gains by 1400
- Ottoman gains by 1451
- Ottoman gains by 1490
- Ottoman vassal states 1490
- 1467 dates of aquisition by the Ottomans
- cities captured by the Ottomans
- ⚔ 1402 battles
- Genoese territory 1490
- Venetian territory 1490
- territory of the Knights of St John (Hospitallers) 1490

The Spread of Printing

The printed book, made possible by the invention of moveable type (c. 1450), allowed the dissemination of the written word on a scale unimaginable even a decade prior to its appearance.

"If it please any man spiritual or temporal to buy [copies of the Sarum Ordinal] imprinted after the form of this present letter, which is well and truly correct, let him come to Westminster into the Almonry at the red pale and he shall have them good chepe."

Earliest advertisement for a book printed by William Caxton, *c.* 1477

Two important strands of European cultural development merged towards the middle of the 15th century to allow the beginning of printing as we know it today. The first was a technological advance: the invention of moveable metal type. Perfected by the goldsmith Johannes Gutenberg in the early 1450s in the German town of Mainz, moveable type allowed pages of text to be laid out and printed quickly and easily for the first time. Each character was now individually cast in metal, allowing it to be used repeatedly with minimal deterioration of print quality and to be replaced within a different text page whenever necessary, two important qualities which traditional woodcut blocks could not emulate. The second development can be connected with the rise of humanism, which espoused the importance of the individual with his or her own will and responsibilities. Humanism in 15th-century northern Europe brought with it increased commercial activity as the former lower classes began to pull themselves up the socio-economic ladder. Rising literacy levels accompanied the new business acumen and fed a growing desire on the part of the public to interpret the world through the written word.

Impact of the Written Word

The development and spread of printing greatly aided this new-found independence. Texts of all kinds could now be mass reproduced for knowledge-hungry consumers. Religious texts, including the Bible, prayer books and sermons, formerly read only by clergy or by a very few wealthy enough to possess lavish and expensive manuscripts, could now be purchased at much lower prices and used by anyone who had mastered the skill of reading. So too could one's political and ethical views be informed by early examples of reform tracts, broadsheets and even printed posters and advertisements. Reading for pleasure now belonged to others outside the royal household and wealthy nobility; histories, romances, poetry and works of fiction appeared with rapidity on the booklists of the early stationers. Academic works were also in demand. Mass printing allowed a single, authorized version of a religious, philosophical or scientific text to be disseminated, while accurate diagrams and illustrations were, for the first time, available to medical students.

From the earliest presses in Mainz, printing spread quickly throughout western Europe, and in the years around 1500 to the East and the New World as well. Germans established presses in central and eastern Europe before 1474, and

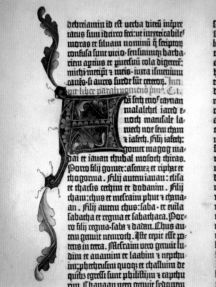

Decorated initial 'A' from the Gutenberg Bible, printed in 1455. The Gutenberg Bible was the first book to be produced using the technique of printing which Johannes Gutenberg (1390–1468) probably invented in the 1450s. Printing was one of the most important technical developments in history.

it is from the Rhineland that printing spread, probably via the Hanseatic port of Lübeck, to Scandinavia, the Baltic States and ultimately to Russia. Printing in Rome began in 1467, several years after a press was opened by Konrad Sweyn-

The Spread of Printing

- ● presses founded before 1460
- ○ presses founded 1470–9
- ● presses founded 1490–9
- ● presses founded 1460–9
- ● presses founded 1480–9
- ——— borders c. 1500

heim and Arnold Pannartz in Subiaco, the location of an important monastic scriptorium just outside of Rome. Paris installed its first press by 1470, when officials from the Sorbonne brought in three German printers to produce university texts. William Caxton, an Englishman who received his training in Germany, opened England's first press in the precincts of Westminster Abbey in 1476; he had previously published *The Recuyell of the Historyes of Troye*, the first book to be printed in the English language (1475), while working in Bruges. Caxton also printed two editions of Chaucer's *Canterbury Tales*. The Iberian Peninsula, whence printing travelled to the New World, possessed numerous presses by 1500, the earliest having been founded in Valencia in Spain around 1473. Portugal lagged behind by a little more than a decade; Eliezer Toledano, a Jewish printer working in Lisbon, published the first Portuguese printed book, a commentary on the Pentateuch, in 1489.

Portuguese Voyages of Discovery

European demand for luxury items from the East increased following the Crusades and the reopening of established trade routes by the Mongols in the 13th century. The Portuguese search for maritime routes to India and China initiated an era of extensive exploration and colonization.

"Portuguese caravels ... were wont to come armed to the Golfo d'Argin ... they took ... both men and women, and carried them to Portugal for sale: behaving in a like manner along all the rest of the coast, which stretches from Cauo Bianco to the Rio di Senega and even beyond."

Edited excerpt from Alvise da Cadamosto, 'Description of Capo Bianco and the Islands Nearest to It'

The great Italian trading ports of Venice and Genoa had established trading posts in the eastern Mediterranean and along the Black Sea coast to aid the transport of goods from Asia into Europe; the Russian Principalities and the Volga Bulgars also jealously guarded their Asian trading depots. The arrival of the Mongols destroyed many social and political institutions, but their subsequent control of the silk and spice roads across Asia fostered increased access to Asian luxury goods for the European market. The unified Mongol state was already unravelling by the late-14th century, making overland trade routes dangerous as newly-formed states struggled for power. At the same time Ottoman *ghazis*, keen on extending Islam across the world, caused further problems for Christian merchants as they conquered Anatolia, much of southeastern Europe and later Palestine, Syria and Egypt. By 1398 the Mongols had been driven from China by Hung-Wu, whose efforts to regain control of China put an end to trade along the Silk Road. With the European economy in trouble, and Venice and Genoa involved in disputes over their colonies in western Asia, the way was open for an enterprising concern to search for new routes to Asia. Portugal, with its maritime traditions, began to look towards North Africa to extend its power.

African Exploration

The Portuguese prince Henry the Navigator is generally credited with spearheading the Portuguese exploration of the African coast. Henry, the third son of King John I of Portugal, was made governor of the Moroccan port of Ceuta when it was captured by the Portuguese in 1415. Henry's aspirations were more spiritual than political; in 1420 he became grand master of the Order of Christ, a secular order which had replaced the Knights Templar in Portugal. Throughout his life, he consistently sponsored voyages along the west coast of Africa, in search of gold, new trading commodities, and peoples who might take up the Christian religion. Henry also had a genuine interest in the discovery of uncharted territories which encouraged him to finance the development of new navigational instruments and cartographic techniques. Henry provided financial sponsorship for many voyages; he backed Gil Eanes who rounded

Portrait of Henry the Navigator (1394–1460) from 'Des Chroniques Chevaleresques de l'Espagne et du Portugal'. Henry was a pioneer of modern exploration; he organized and funded the voyages of discovery which led to the rounding of Africa and the establishment of a sea route to the Indies.

Cape Bojador (1434) and Dinis Dias who discovered the mouth of the Sénégal River (1445). By his death in 1460, Portuguese navigators had explored the west coast of Africa at least as far as modern Sierra Leone, and Portugal laid claim to

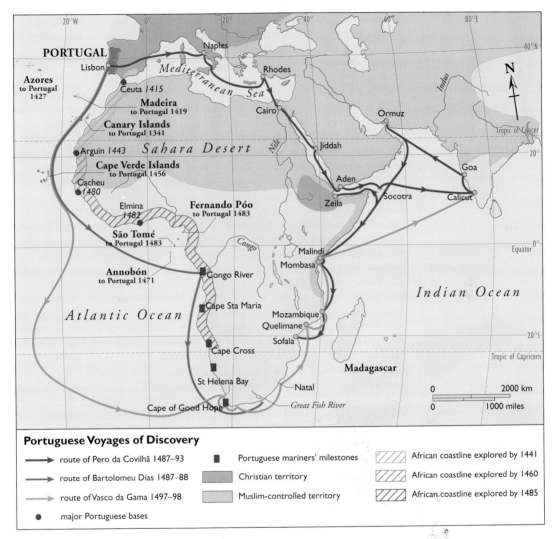

Portuguese Voyages of Discovery

→ route of Pero da Covilhã 1487–93

→ route of Bartolomeu Dias 1487–88

→ route of Vasco da Gama 1497–98

● major Portuguese bases

■ Portuguese mariners' milestones

Christian territory

Muslim-controlled territory

African coastline explored by 1441

African coastline explored by 1460

African coastline explored by 1485

numerous colonies on the African mainland as well as to the Azores, Madeira, and the Canary and Cape Verde Islands. By 1450 Portuguese coffers were filling with gold from Africa and income from trade in African slaves.

Other Portuguese Achievements

Portuguese exploration continued after Henry's death. In 1469 Fernão Gomes was granted a trade monopoly on the western coast of Africa in exchange for continuing to chart the African coast. Diogo Cão erected milestones to indicate Portuguese control at the mouth of the Congo River and at Cape Santa Maria (1482), and later at Cape Cross (1485). In 1487 Pero de Covilha left Lisbon in search of a route to India through eastern Africa; he reached Cannanore, Calicut and Goa. Bartolomeu Dias rounded the Cape of Good Hope in 1488. A decade later, Vasco da Gama sailed around Africa and across the Indian Ocean, thus opening a sea route from Europe to India.

The First Voyages to the New World

Christopher Columbus, an experienced navigator in search of a western route to China and India, successfully crossed the Atlantic Ocean in 1492. By 1525 the Americas were recognized as distinct from Asia, and the exploration and colonization of the New World was underway.

> "*They saw many kinds of trees and plants and fragrant flowers; they saw birds of many kinds, different from those of Spain .... Four-footed beasts they did not see, except dogs that did not bark.*"
>
> Entry for 6 November 1492 from the Journal of Christopher Columbus

The four journeys to the New World undertaken by Columbus were largely funded by the Spanish rulers Ferdinand II and Isabella I, whose marital alliance unified Aragon, Castile and Leon into what would become the kingdom of Spain. Jealous of Portugal's new-found wealth and African colonies, and buoyed up by the capitulation of the last Muslim stronghold in Spain, Ferdinand and Isabella were eager to extend their territories and increase their revenues.

Columbus' Early Voyages

Columbus, Genoese by birth, had trained in the Portuguese merchant navy, but refusal of sponsorship by John II of Portugal led him to approach the Spanish for support. His first crossing took just over two months; he is generally thought to have landed on San Salvador (Watling Island) in the Bahamas. Believing that he was very close to China, he went on to discover Cuba and Hispaniola (modern Haiti and the Dominican Republic). On his second voyage, Columbus charted the Lesser Antilles, the Virgin Islands and Jamaica, before returning to Hispaniola to visit his garrison there and to add to the gold, spices, herbs and slaves that he had earlier taken back to Spain. Subsequently Columbus landed on Trinidad, Martinique, as well as on Central and South America, where he explored the mouth of the Orinoco River. Although his explorations and navigational skills were highly valued by the Spanish, Columbus did not enjoy the honours and financial rewards that he had hoped for. His ineptitude at governing settlements and commanding his crews added to growing concerns about the relatively low profits returned by his voyages. His Italian background further fomented Spanish resentment. In the New World his dogged, sometimes crude attempts to convert indigenous peoples to Christianity and his endless need to procure booty for himself and to impress his sponsors endeared him neither to native inhabitants nor to Spanish settlers.

Christopher Columbus may have initiated European discovery of the New World, but many other individuals participated in early exploratory expeditions. Rodrigo de Bastidas, Juan de la Cosa and Vasco Núñez de Balboa explored the Isthmus of Panama in 1499. By the end of 1502, Amerigo Vespucci, working first for Spain and later Portugal, had seen the Amazon and followed the South American Coast at least as far south as the mouth of the Rio Platte. Spain's successes in the New World prompted much

Portrait of Christopher Columbus attributed to Sebastian del Piombo (c. 1485–1547). It was painted in 1519, but there is some doubt as to whether Piombo created this picture or, indeed, if it is actually of Columbus.

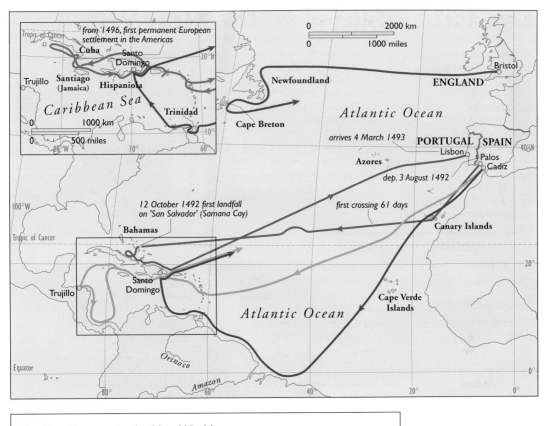

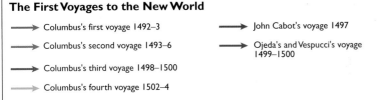

The First Voyages to the New World

→ Columbus's first voyage 1492–3

→ Columbus's second voyage 1493–6

→ Columbus's third voyage 1498–1500

→ Columbus's fourth voyage 1502–4

→ John Cabot's voyage 1497

→ Ojeda's and Vespucci's voyage 1499–1500

admiration and envy among European powers. Sailing for England, the Venetian John Cabot set out to find a route to Asia over the north Atlantic, exploring the Canadian coast in the late 1490s. The Portuguese, already established in Africa, began to look west; Pedro Álvares Cabral would discover Brazil in 1500. In 1494 the Spanish, with papal backing, drafted the treaty of Tordesillas, which awarded Portugal the rights to all newly-discovered territories up to 100 leagues west of the Cape Verde Islands, with everything further west to belong to Spain. Among the European states, only Portugal signed up; disputes over the details of the treaty arose almost immediately.

Spain's new possessions increased Spanish territory, revenues and prestige immensely. The cost to the indigenous peoples of the New World, however, cannot be overlooked. Spain, and, over time, other European powers, systematically destroyed ancient civilizations – some very advanced – through massacres, forcible conversion and strict implementation of European political and social structures. Much of what the New World could supply greatly enriched European culture and finances; other legacies from the New World, such as syphilis and tobacco, would not prove so beneficial.

Dynastic Tables

Medieval Popes from the Revival of the Empire

Leo III 795-816
Stephen IV 816-7
Paschal I 817-24
Eugene II 824-7
Valentine 827
Gregory IV 827-44
John (antipope) 844
Sergius II 844-7
Leo IV 847-55
Benedict III 855-8
Anastasius Bibliothecarius (antipope) 855
Nicholas I 858-67
Hadrian II 867-72
John VIII 872-82
Marinus I 882-4
Hadrian III 884-5
Stephen V 885-91
Formosus 891-6
Boniface VI 896
Stephen VI 896-7
Romanus 897
Theodore II 897
John IX 898-900
Benedict IV 900-3
Leo V 903
Christopher (antipope) 903-4
Sergius III 904-11
Anastasius III 911-3
Lando 913-4
John X 914-28
Leo VI 928
Stephen VII 928-31
John XI 931-35
Leo VII 936-9
Stephen VIII 939-42
Marinus II 942-6
Agapitus II 946-55
John XII 955-64
Leo VIII 963-5
Benedict V 964
John XIII 965-72
Benedict VI 973-4
Boniface (VII) (antipope) 974; 984-5
Benedict VII 974-83
John XIV 983-4
John XV 985-96
Gregory V 996-9
John (XVI) (antipope) 997-8
Silvester II 999-1003
John XVII 1003
John XVIII 1003-9
Sergius IV 1009-12
Benedict VIII 1012-24
Gregory (VI) (antipope) 1012
John XIX 1024-32

Benedict IX 1032-44; 1045; 1047-8
Silvester III 1045
Gregory VI 1045-6
Clement II 1046-7
Damasus II 1048
Leo IX 1049-54
Victor II 1055-7
Stephen IX 1057-8
Benedict (X) (antipope) 1058-9
Nicholas II 1058-61
Alexander II 1061-73
Honorius (II) (antipope) 1061-4
Gregory VII 1073-85
Clement (III) (antipope) 1080; 1100
Victor III 1086; 1087
Urban II 1088-99
Paschal II 1099-1118
Theodoric (antipope) 1100-1
Adalbert (antipope) 1101
Silvester (IV) (antipope) 1105-11
Gelasius II 1118-19
Gregory (VIII) (antipope) 1118-21
Callistus II 1119-24
Honorius II 1124-30
Clestine II 1124
Innocent II 1130-43
Anacletus (II) (antipope) 1130-8
Victor (IV) (antipope) 1138
Celestine II 1143-4
Lucius II 1144-5
Eugene III 1145-53
Anastasius IV 1153-4
Hadrian IV 1154-9
Alexander III 1159-81
Victor IV (antipope) 1159-64
Paschal (III) (antipope) 1164-8
Callistus (III) (antipope) 1168-78
Innocent (III) (antipope) 1179-80
Lucius III 1181-5
Urban III 1185-7
Gregory VIII 1187
Clement III 1187-91
Celestine III 1191-8
Innocent III 1198-1216
Honorius III 1216-27
Gregory IX 1227-41
Celestine IV 1241
Innocent IV 1243-1254
Alexander IV 1254-61
Urban IV 1261-4
Clement IV 1265-8
Gregory X 1271-6
Innocent V 1276
Hadrian V 1276
John XXI 1276-7
Nicholas III 1277-80
Martin IV 1281-5

Honorius IV 1285-7
Nicholas IV 1288-92
Celestine V 1294
Boniface VIII 1294-1303
Benedict XI 1303-4
Clement V 1305-14
John XXII 1316-34
Nicholas (V) (antipope) 1328-30
Benedict XII 1334-42
Clement VI 1342-52
Innocent VI 1352-62
Urban V 1362-70
Grgeory XI 1370-8
Urban VI 1378-89
Clement (VII) (antipope) 1378-94
Boniface IX 1389-1404
Benedict (XIII) (antipope) 1394-1417
Innocent VII 1404-6
Gregory XII 1406-15
Alexander (V) (antipope) 1409-10
John (XXIII) (antipope) 1410-15
Martin V 1417-31
Clement (VIII) (antipope) 1423-9
Benedict (XIV) (antipope) 1425-?
Eugene IV 1431-47
Felix (V) (antipope) 1439-1449
Nicholas V 1447-55
Callistus III 1455-8
Pius II 1458-64
Paul II 1464-71
Sixtus IV 1471-84
Innocent VIII 1484-92
Alexander VI 1492-1503

German Kings and Holy Roman Emperors

Conrad I 911-8
Henry I the Fowler 919-36
Otto I the Great 936-73; Emp. 962-73
Otto II 973-83; Emp. 973-83
Otto III 983-1002; Emp. 996-1002
Henry II 1002-24; Emp. 1014-24
Conrad II 1024-39; Emp. 1027-39
Henry III 1039-56; Emp. 1046-56
Henry IV 1056-1106; Emp. 1084-1105
Henry V 1106-25; Emp. 1111-25
Lothair II 1125-37; Emp. 1133-7
Conrad III 1138-52
Frederick I Barbarossa 1152-90;
  Emp. 1155-90
Henry VI 1190-7; Emp. 1191-7
Philip of Swabia 1198-1208
Otto IV of Brunswick 1208-1218;
  Emp. 1209-1218
Frederick II 1212-50 (Emp. 1220-1245)
Conrad IV 1250-4

William II of Holland 1247-56
Alfonso X of Castile 1257-73
Richard of Cornwall 1257-72
Rudolf I of Habsburg 1273-91
Adolf of Nassau-Weilburg 1292-8
    (Dep. 1298)
Albert I of Habsburg 1298-1308
Henry VII of Luxemburg 1309-13
    Emp. 1311-3
Louis IV of Bavaria 1314-47;
    Emp. 1328-47
Charles IV of Luxemburg 1347-78;
    Emp. 1355-78
Wenceslas of Luxemburg 1378-1400
Rupert III of Bavaria 1400-10
Sigismund of Luxemburg 1410-37;
    Emp. 1433-7
Albert II of Habsburg 1438-9
Frederick III 1440-93; Emp. 1452-93
Maximilian I 1493-1519 (Emp. Elect
    from 1508)

Kings of France

Capetians:
Hugh Capet 987-96
Robert II the Pious 996-1031
Henry I 1031-60
Philip I 1060-1108
Louis VI 1108-37
Louis VII 1137-80
Philip II Augustus 1180-1223
Louis VIII 1223-6
Louis IX (Saint Louis) 1226-70
Philip III 1270-85
Philip IV the Fair 1285-1314
Louis X 1314-6
John I 1316
Philip V 1316-22
Charles IV 1322-8
House of Valois:
Philip VI 1328-50
John II the Good 1350-64
Charles V the Wise 1364-80
Charles VI 1380-1422
Charles VII 1422-61
Louis XI 1461-83
Charles VIII 1483-98

Kings of England

Alfred the Great 871-99
Edward the Elder 899-925
Athelstan 925-40
Edmund I 940-6
Edred 946-55
Edwy 955-9
Edgar 959-75
Edward the Martyr 975-8
Ethelred II 978-1016

Edmund Ironside 1016-7
Canute 1017-35
Harold I Harefoot 1035-40
Hardicanute 1040-2
Edward the Confessor 1042-66
Harold II Godwinson 1066
House of Normandy:
William I the Conqueror 1066-87
William II Rufus 1087-1100
Henry I 1100-35
Stephen 1135-54
Plantagenets:
Henry II 1154-89
Richard I Lionheart 1189-99
John 1199-1216
Henry III 1216-72
Edward I 1272-1307
Edward II 1307-27
Edward III 1327-77
Richard II 1377-99
House of Lancaster:
Henry IV 1399-1413
Henry V 1413-22
Henry VI 1422-61
House of York:
Edward IV 1461-83
Edward V 1483
Richard III 1483-5
House of Tudor:
Henry VII 1485-1509

Byzantine Emperors the Iconoclastic Controversy

Isaurean Dynasty:
Leo III the Isaurian 717-41
Constantine V Copronymus 741, 743-75
Artabasdus (rival emperor) 741-3
Leo IV the Khazar 775-80
Constantine VI the Blinded 780-97
Irene the Athenian 797-802
Nicephorus I the General Logothete
    802-11
Stauracius 811
Michael I Rhangabe 811-3
Leo V the Armenian 813-20
Amorian (Phrygian) Dynasty:
Michael II the Amorian 820-9
Theophilus II 829-42
Michael III 842-67
Macedonian Dynasty:
Basil I the Macedonian 867-86
Leo VI the Wise 886-912
Alexander III 912-3
Constantine VII Porphyrogenitus 913-59
Romanus I Lecapenus (co-emperor)
    919-44
Romanus II Porphyrogentius 959-63
Nicephorus II Phocas 963-9
John I Tzimisces 969-76

Basil II Bulgaroktonus 976-1025
Constantine VIII Porphyrogentius 1025-8
Romanus III Argyrus 1028-34
Michael IV the Paphlagonian 1034-41
Michael V Calaphates 1041-2
Constantine IX Monomachus 1042-54
Theodora Porphyrogenita 1054-6
Michael VI Stratioticus 1056-7
Proto-Comnenan Dynasty:
Isaac I Comnenus 1057-9
Constantine X Ducas 1059-67
Michael VII Ducas 1067-78
Romanus IV Diogenes (co-emperor)
    1067-71
Nicephorus III Botaniates 1078-81
Comnenan Dynasty:
Alexius I Comnenus 1081-1118
John II Comnenus 1118-43
Manuel I Comnenus 1143-80
Alexius II Comnenus 1180-3
Andronicus I Comnenus 1183-5
Angelan Dynasty:
Isaac II Angelus 1185-95
Alexius III Angelus 1195-1203
Alexius IV Angelus 1203-4
Isaac II Angelus (restored with Alexius IV)
    1203-4
Alexius V Ducas Murzuphlus 1204
*Lascaran Dynasty (in exile as the
empire of Nicaea):*
Theodore I Lascaris 1204-22
John III Ducas Vatatzes 1222-54
Theodore II Lascaris 1254-8
John IV Lascaris 1258-61
*Palaeologan Dynasty (restored at
Constantinople):*
Michael VIII Palaeologus 1259-82
Andronicus II Palaeologus 1282-1328
Andronicus III Palaeologus 1328-41
John V Palaeologus 1341-76, 1379-91
John VI Cantacuzenus (co-emperor)
    1347-54
Andronicus IV Palaeologus 1376-9
John VII Palaeologus (rival emperor) 1390
Manuel II Palaeologus 1391-1425
John VII Palaeologus (rival emperor)
    1399-1402
John VIII Palaeologus 1425-48
Constantine XI Palaeologus 1449-53

Latin Emperors of Constantinople

Baldwin I 1204-5
Henry of Flanders 1206-16
Peter of Courtenay 1217
Yolanda of Flanders 1217-1219
Robert of Courtenay 1221-8
Baldwin II 1228-61

Further reading

I. GENERAL

Barber, Malcolm, *The Two Cities: Medieval Europe 1050–1320* (London, 1992)

Bartlett, Robert, *The Making of Europe: Conquest, Civilisation and Cultural Change 950–1350* (Harmondsworth, 1994)

Brown, Peter, *The Rise of Western Christendom: Triumph and Diversity 200–1000* (Oxford, 2002)

Collins, Roger, *Early Medieval Europe, 300–1000* (Basingstoke, 1991)

Holmes, George, *Europe: Hierarchy and Revolt, 1320–1450* (Oxford, 2000)

Jordan, William C., *Europe in the High Middle Ages* (London, 2001)

Le Goff, Jacques, *Medieval Civilization* (Oxford, 1988)

Mundy, John, *Europe in the High Middle Ages, 1150–1300* (Harlow, 2000)

2. RELIGION AND THE CHURCH

Hamilton, Bernard, *Religion in the Medieval West* (London, 2003)

Lawrence, C.H., *Medieval Monasticism* (Harlow, 2001)

Morris, Colin, *The Papal Monarchy* (Oxford, 1989)

Southern, Richard, *Western Society and the Church in the Middle Ages* (Harmondsworth, 1970)

Swanson, Robert, *Religion and Devotion in Europe 1215–1515* (Cambridge, 1995)

Thomson, J.A.F., *The Western Church in the Middle Ages* (London, 1998)

Webb, Diana, *Medieval European Pilgrimage, c. 700–c. 1500* (Basingstoke, 2002)

3. LORDSHIP AND GOVERNMENT

Bartlett, Robert, *England under the Norman and Angevin Kings 1075–1225* (Oxford, 2000)

Bloch, Marc, *Feudal Society* (London, 1961)

Dunbabin, Jean, *France in the Making* (Oxford, 1985)

Frame, Robin, *The Political Development of the British Isles, 1100–1400* (Oxford, 1990)

Hallam, Elizabeth, *Capetian France* (London, 1980)

Poly, J-P and Bournazel, E., *The Feudal Transformation, 900–1200* (New York, 1991)

4. EUROPEAN EXPANSION

Christiansen, Eric, *The Northern Crusades* (Harmondsworth, 1997)

Jotischky, Andrew, *Crusading and the Crusader States* (Harlow, 2004)

O'Callaghan, Joseph, *Reconquest and Crusade in Medieval Spain* (Philadephia, 2002)

Richard, Jean, *The Crusades* (Cambridge, 1999)

Riley-Smith, Jonathan, *What Were the Crusades?* (Basingstoke, 2002)

5. WARFARE, CHIVALRY AND COURT CULTURE

Contamine, Phillipe, *War in the Middle Ages* (Oxford, 1984)

Duby, Georges, *The Chivalrous Society* (London, 1979)

Barber, Richard, *The Knight and Chivalry* (London, 1970)

DeVries, Kelly, *Medieval Military Technology* (Peterborough, Ontario, 1992)

Keen, Maurice, *Chivalry* (New Haven, 1984)

6. THE MEDIEVAL ECONOMY

Duby, Georges, *Rural Economy and Country Life in the Medieval West* (Columbia, 1968)

Gimpel, Jean, *The Medieval Machine: The Industrial Revolution of the Middle Ages* (London, 1992)

Spufford, Peter, *Money and its Uses in Medieval Europe* (Cambrige, 1987)

Spufford, Peter, *Power and Profit: The Merchant in Medieval Europe* (London, 2002)

Index

Acknowledgements

PICTURE CREDITS

Pages: 8–9 The Bridgeman Art Library, London/ Biblioteque National, Paris; 14 Scala, Florence/ Bargello, Florence; 15 Scala, Florence/British Library; 16 Scala, Florence; 18 Werner Forman Archives/National Museum, Copenhagen; 19 Corbis/Archivio Iconografico, S.A.; 21 Werner Forman Archives/National Museum, Rome; 22 John Haywood; 25 Paul Coulton; 26 Scala, Florence; 28–30 John Haywood; 35–9 Scala, Florence; 40 The Bridgeman Art Library, London/ Biblioteca Apostolica Vaticana, The Vatican; 42 AKG, London; 44–6 The Bridgeman Art Library, London; 49 *t* John Haywood; *b* Scala, Florence/Church of the Martorana, Palermo; 50 The Bridgeman Art Library, London; 53 Scala, Florence/Magyar Nemzeti Galeria, Budapest; 54 Scala, Florence/San Francesco, Assisi; 55–9 John Haywood; 60–2 The Bridgeman Art Library, London; 65 John Haywood; 66 Bildarchiv Preussischer Kulturbesitz (BPK), Germany; 68 Scala, Florence/Santa Trinita, Florence; 70 Scala, Florence/ Ducal Palace, Urbino; 72 Scala, Florence/Laurentian Library, Florence; 75 Skyscan; 77 The Bridgeman Art Library, London/Musée Condé, Chantilly; 78 AKG, London/Eric Lessing; 80 AKG, London/Heidelberg University Library; 82 John Haywood; 85 Scala, Florence; 86 The Bridgeman Art Library, London; 87 Corbis/David Bartruff; 89 The Bridgeman Art Library, London/Duomo, Monreale, Sicily; 91 Werner Forman Archives; 92 John Swift; 94 Scala, Florence; 96 Scala, Florence; 98 The Bridgeman Art Library, London/British Museum, London; 101 The Bridgeman Art Library, London; 102 Scala, Florence/British Library; 105 *t* AISA; *b* Simon Hall; 106 AKG, London; 108–11 AISA; 113 Scala, Florence/British Library; 114 The Bridgeman Art Library, London/Private collection; 115 The Bridgeman Art Library, London; 116 The Bridgeman Art Library, London/British Library, London; 119 Scala, Florence/Louvre; 120 Werner Forman Archives; 123 AKG, London/Hamburg City Archive; 125 Simon Hall; 126 Scala, Florence; 128 The Bridgeman Art Library, London; 130 The Bridgeman Art Library, London/Universitäts-bibliothek, Göttingen; 134 The Bridgeman Art Library, London/Metropolitan Museum of Art, New York.

Conceived and produced by John Haywood and Simon Hall
Designed by Darren Bennett
Edited by Fiona Plowman
Picture research by Veneta Bullen
Cartography by Tim Aspden and the University of Southampton
    Cartography Unit

... a Haywood & Hall production for Penguin Books